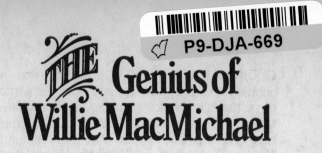

The Genius of Willie MacMichael

P9-DJA-669

The Genius of Willie MacMichael

GEORGE MACDONALD

Edited for today's young reader by
DAN HAMILTON

A WINNER BOOK

VICTOR BOOKS®

A DIVISION OF SCRIPTURE PRESS PUBLICATIONS INC.
USA CANADA ENGLAND

WINNER BOOKS BY GEORGE MACDONALD:
The Boyhood of Ranald Bannerman
The Genius of Willie MacMichael
The Wanderings of Clare Skymer

Second printing, 1988

Library of Congress Catalog Card Number: 86-63100
ISBN: 0-89693-750-X

VICTOR BOOKS
A division of SP Publications, Inc.
Wheaton, Illinois 60187

CONTENTS

George MacDonald wrote his many books for the childlike of all ages—for any man, woman, boy, or girl who would receive God, the things of God, and the things of God's world with open hands, warm hearts, and simple faith.

The Genius of Willie MacMichael is one such book, originally published in 1873 as *Gutta Percha Willie: The Working Genius.* In telling this tale, MacDonald drew from events of his own boyhood in Scotland and from his own keen interest in things mechanical and chemical and natural. Willie's dilemma reflects the problem MacDonald faced in 1845, when he had graduated from King's College in Aberdeen and did not know what to do next. He was interested in chemistry, natural philosophy, poetry, medicine, and the ministry, but had no clear path before him. He chose first a tutor's position and later, for a time, the formal ministry; his ultimate free-lance writing and speaking career would encompass both the sciences and the arts without neglecting the message of the Gospel.

Like many other authors of his time, MacDonald did have some technical faults as a writer. Yet he was a true *storyteller,* and always left his audience turning pages to see what would happen next. His narrative skill was matched by the wise quality of his insights into the heart of the living God, for MacDonald spun his tales in order to tell us all about our Heavenly Father, His Son and our brother Jesus Christ, and the unbounded love with which They seek to persuade us to turn from our sin into Their open arms.

This special edition has been slightly trimmed from the original and clarified for fuller enjoyment. May it bring all its readers delight in a "new" author, and spur a growing interest in MacDonald at his fullest and best. And may such interest warrant the eventual reprinting of his complete, original works.

DAN HAMILTON

CHAPTER ONE
Willie

The boy's real name was Willie, for his father and mother gave it to him—not William, but Willie MacMichael. It was his own father, however, who gave him the name of Gutta-Percha Willie, the reason of which will also show itself by and by.

Dr. MacMichael was a country doctor, living in a small village in a thinly peopled country. He had very hard work, for he often had to ride many miles to see a patient, and frequently in the middle of the night. And for this hard work he had very little pay, for a thinly peopled country is generally a poor country, and those who live in it are poor also, and cannot spend much even upon their health. Although he would have been glad to have richer patients, and closer to each other, he not only preferred a country life, but he would say to anyone who expressed surprise that with his reputation he should remain where he was, "What's to become of my little flock if I go away? There are very few doctors of my experience who would come and undertake my work. I know every man, woman, and child in the whole countryside, and that makes all the difference." He was a good kindhearted man who loved his work, for the sake of those whom he helped by it, better than the money he received for it.

Their home was necessarily a very humble one—a neat little cottage in the village of Priory Leas—almost the one pretty spot thereabout. It lay in a valley in the midst of hills, which did not look high, because they rose with a gentle slope and had no bold elevations or grand-shaped peaks. But they rose to a good height notwithstanding, and the weather on the top of them in the wintertime was often bitter and fierce—bitter with keen frost, and fierce with wild winds. Of both frost and wind the village at their feet had its share too, but of course they were not so bad down below, for the hills were a shelter from the wind, and it is always colder the farther you go up and away from the heart of this ball of rock and earth upon which we live. When Willie's father was riding across the great moorland of those desolate hills, and the people in the village would be saying to each other how bitterly cold it was, he would be thinking how snug and warm it was down there, and how nice it would be to turn a certain corner on the road back and slip at once out of the freezing wind that had it all its own way up among the withered gorse and heather.

For his part, Willie cared very little what the weather was, but took it as it came. In the hot summer, he would lie in the long grass and get cool, and in the cold winter, he would scamper about and get warm. When his hands were as cold as icicles, his cheeks would be red as apples. When his mother took his hands in hers and chafed them, full of pity for their suffering, as she thought it, Willie first knew that they were cold by the sweet warmth of the kind hands that chafed them: he had not thought of it before. Climbing among the ruins of the Priory,* or playing with Farmer Thomson's boys and girls about the ricks* in his yard, in the thin clear saffron twilight which came so early after noon, when, to some people, every breath seemed full of needle-points, so sharp was the cold, he was comfortable and

---

*You can find an explanation of the starred words in the Glossary, pages 161-163.

happy as if he had been a creature of the winter only and found himself quite at home in it.

There were large ruins which they called the Priory. It was not often that monks chose such a poor country to settle in, but I suppose they had their reasons. And I daresay they were not monks at all, but begging friars, who founded it when they wanted to reprove the luxury and greed of the monks; and perhaps by the time they had grown as bad themselves, the place was nearly finished and they could not well move it. They had chosen the one pretty spot in the valley, where the land was tolerably good, and grew excellent oats if poor wheat, while the gardens were equal to apples and a few pears, besides an abundance of gooseberries, currants, and strawberries.

The ruins of the Priory lay behind Dr. MacMichael's cottage—indeed, in the very garden. The place was his own, so long as he paid a small sum—fifteen shillings* a year—to his superior. How long it was since the Priory had been looked upon as the mere encumbrance of a cottage garden, nobody thereabout knew, and nobody except its owner had then taken the trouble to make the least inquiry into its history. To Willie, it was just the Priory, as naturally in his father's garden as if every garden had similar ruins.

The ruins were of considerable extent, with remains of Gothic arches, and carvings about the doors—all open to the sky except a few vaulted places on the ground level. These were perfectly solid, and were used by the family to store wood and peats* and garden tools. In summer, golden flowers grew on the broken walls, and in winter, gray frosts edged them against the sky.

The whole garden was but the space once occupied by the huge building, for its surface was most irregular. It was up and down, up and down in whatever direction you went, mounded with heaps of ruins, over which the mold had gathered. For many years bushes and flowers had grown upon them, and you might dig a good way without coming to the stones, though come to them you must at last. The walks wound about between the heaps, and through the thick walls of the ruin, overgrown with lichens* and mosses, now and then passing through an arched door or window of the ancient building. It was a generous garden in old-fashioned flowers and vegetables. There were a few apple and pear trees also on a wall that faced the south, which were regarded by Willie with mingled respect and desire, for he was not allowed to touch them, while of the gooseberries he was allowed to eat as many as he pleased when they were ripe, and of currants too, after his mother had had as many as she wanted for preserves. But some spots were much too shady to allow either fruit or flowers to grow in them, so high and close were the walls.

CHAPTER TWO

Willie's Education

Willie was more than nine years of age before he could read a single word. It was not that he was stupid, but that he had not learned the good of reading, and therefore had not begun to wish to read. His father had unusual ideas about how Willie ought to be educated, and said he would no more think of making Willie learn to read before he wished to be taught than he would make him eat if he wasn't hungry. The gift of reading, he said, was too good a thing to give him before he wished to have it, or knew the value of it. "Would you give him a watch," he would say, "before he cares to know whether the sun rises in the east or the west, or at what hour dinner will be ready?"

This might not work with some boys and girls, but it worked well in Willie's case, who was neither lazy nor idle. And it must not be supposed that he was left without any education at all. For one thing, his father and mother used to talk very freely before him—and nothing serves better for teaching than the conversation of good and thoughtful people. While they talked, Willie would listen intently, trying to understand what he heard; and although it frequently took very strange shapes in his little mind, because at times he understood neither the words nor the things the words represented, yet there was much that he did understand and make good use of.

Willie soon came to know that his father and mother had very little money to spare, and that his father had to work hard to get what money they had. He learned also that everything that came into the house, or was done for them, cost money; therefore, for one thing, he must not ill-use his clothes. He learned too that there was a great deal of suffering in the world, and that his father's business was to try to make it less, and help people who were ill to grow well again, and be able to do their work. This made Willie see what a useful man his father was, and wish to be also of some good in the world. Then he looked about him and saw that there were a great many ways of getting money, that is, a great many things for doing which people would give money; and he saw that some of those ways were better than others, and he thought his father's way the very best of all.

And he had another teacher. Down the street of the straggling village, with nearly as many little gardens as houses in it, there was a house occupied by several poor people. In one end of the house, in just a room and a closet, an old woman lived who made her money by spinning flax into yarn for making linen. Mrs. Wilson was a kindhearted old creature—a widow, without any relation near to help her or look after her. She had had a Willie of her own, her child who died before he was as old as Willie MacMichael. That was forty years before, but she had never forgotten her own little Willie, and she fancied that this Willie was like him. Nothing, therefore, pleased her better than to get him into her little room and talk to him. She would take a little bit of sugar candy or licorice out of her cupboard for him, and tell him some strange old fairy tale or legend while she sat spinning, until at last she had made him so fond of her that he would often stay for hours with her.

Nor did it make much difference when his mother begged Mrs. Wilson to give him something sweet only now and then, for she was afraid of his going to see the old woman merely for what she gave him, which would have been greedy. But the fact was, he liked her stories better than her sugar candy and licorice, while above all things he delighted in watching the wonderful wheel go round and round so fast that he could not find out whether her foot was making it spin or it was making her foot dance up and down in that curious way.

After she had explained it to him as well as she could, and he thought he understood it, it seemed to him only the more wonderful and mysterious. And ever as it went whirring round, it sung a song of its own, which was also the song of the story that the old woman was telling him, as he sat listening in her high soft chair, covered with long-faded chintz,* and cushioned like a nest. For Mrs. Wilson had had a better house to live in once, and this chair, as well as the chest of drawers of dark mahogany, with brass handles, that stood opposite the window, was part of the furniture she saved when she had to sell the rest. In her chair, the little boy would sit coiled up as nearly into a ball as might be, like a young bird or rabbit in its nest, staring at the wheel, and listening with two ears and one heart to its song and the old woman's tale both at once.

One sultry afternoon, Willie's mother was not very well and had gone to lie down; his father was out, as he so often was, upon Scramble the old horse; and Tibby, their only servant, was busy with the ironing. Willie ran off to Widow Wilson's, and was soon curled up in the chair, like a little Hindu idol that had grown weary of sitting upright, and had tumbled itself into a corner.

Now, before he came, the old woman had been thinking about him, and wishing very much that he would come. She was turning over also in her mind, as she spun, all her stock of stories, in the hope of finding in some nook or other, one she had not yet told him. Although he had not yet begun to grow tired even of those he knew best, it was a special treat to have a new one; for by this time Mrs. Wilson's store was all but exhausted, and a new one turned up very rarely. This time, however, she was successful, and did call to mind one that she had not thought of before. It had not only grown very dusty, but was full of little holes, which she at once set about darning up with the needle and thread of her imagination, so that by the time Willie arrived, she had a treat, as she thought, quite ready for him.

The story was about a poor boy who received from a fairy to whom he had shown some kindness the gift of a marvelous wand, in the shape of a common blackthorn walking stick, which nobody could suspect of possessing such wonderful virtue. By means of it, he was able to do anything he wished without the least trouble. So upon a trial of skill, appointed by a certain king, in order to find out which of the craftsmen of his realm was fittest to aid him in ruling it, he found it easy to surpass every one of them, each in his own trade. He produced a richer damask* than any of the silk weavers; a finer linen than any of the linen weavers; a more complicated as well as ornate cabinet with more drawers and quaint hiding places than any of the cabinetmakers; a sword blade more cunningly damasked, and a hilt more gorgeously jeweled than any of the sword makers; a ring set with stones more precious, more brilliant in color, and more beautifully combined, than any of the jewelers. In short, without knowing a single device of one of the arts in question, he surpassed every one of the competitors in his own craft, won the favor of the king and the office he wished to confer, and gained at length the king's daughter to boot.

For a long time Willie had not uttered a single exclamation, and when the old woman looked up, fancying he must be asleep, she saw, to her disappointment, a cloud upon his face—amounting to a frown.

"What's the matter with you, Willie?" she asked. "Have you got a headache?"

"No, Mrs. Wilson," answered Willie, "but I don't like that story at all."

"I'm sorry for that. I thought I should be sure to please you this time. It is one I never told you before, for I had quite forgotten it myself till this very afternoon. Why don't you like it?"

"Because he was a cheat. *He* couldn't do those things—it was only the fairy's wand that did them."

"But he was such a good lad, and had been so kind to the fairy."

"That makes no difference. He *wasn't* good. And the fairy wasn't good either, or she wouldn't have set him to do such wicked things."

"They weren't wicked things. They were all first-rate—better than anyone else could make them."

"But he didn't *make* them. There wasn't one of those poor fellows he cheated that wasn't a better man than he. The worst of them could do something with his own hands, and I don't believe he could do anything, for if he had ever tried he would have hated to be such a sneak. He cheated the king too, and the princess, and everybody. Oh! Shouldn't I like to have been there, and to have beaten him wand and all! For somebody might have been able to make the things better still, if he had only known how."

Mrs. Wilson was disappointed, and perhaps a little ashamed that she had not thought of this before. She grew cross, and because she was cross, she grew unfair and said to Willie, "You think a great deal of yourself, Master Willie! Pray what could those idle little hands of yours do, if you were to try?"

"I don't know, for I haven't tried," answered Willie.

"It's a pity you shouldn't," she rejoined, "if you think they would turn out so very clever."

She didn't mean anything but crossness when she said this, but Willie took her up quite seriously, and asked in a tone that showed he wanted it accounted for, "Why haven't I ever done anything, Mrs. Wilson?"

"You ought to know that best yourself," she answered, still cross. "I suppose because you don't like to work. Your good father and mother work very hard, I'm sure. It's a shame of you to be so idle."

This was rather hard on a boy of seven, for Willie was no more then. It made him look very grave indeed, if not unhappy for a little while, as he sat turning over the thing in his mind.

"Is it wrong to play about, Mrs. Wilson?" he asked, after a pause of considerable duration.

"No, indeed, my dear," she answered. During the pause she had begun to be sorry for having spoken so roughly to her little darling.

"Does everybody work?"

"Everybody that's worth anything, and is old enough," she added.

"Does God work?" he asked, after another pause, in a low voice.

"No, child. What should He work for?"

"If everybody works that is good and old enough, then I think God must work," answered Willie. "But I will ask my papa. Am I old enough?"

"Well, you're not old enough to do much, but you might do something."

"What could I do? Could I spin, Mrs. Wilson?"

"No, child, that's not an easy thing to do. But you could knit."

"Could I? What good would it do?"

"Why, you could knit your mother a pair of stockings."

"Could I though? Will you teach me, Mrs. Wilson?"

Mrs. Wilson very readily promised, foreseeing that she might have a good deal more of the little man's company, if indeed he was earnest. She was very lonely, and was never so happy as when Willie was with her. She said she would get him some knitting needles—wires she called them—that very evening. She had some wool, and if he came tomorrow, she would soon see whether he was old enough and clever enough to learn to knit. She advised him, however, to say nothing about it to his mother, for he could then surprise her by taking her something of his own knitting, at least a pair of muffetees* to keep her wrists warm in the winter. Willie went home with his solemn secret.

The next day he began to learn, and although his fingers annoyed him a good deal at first by refusing to do exactly as he wanted them, they soon became more obedient. Before the new year arrived, he had actually knitted a pair of warm white lambswool stockings for his mother. When first finished they were a good deal soiled by having been on the way so long, and perhaps partly by the little hands not always being so clean as they might have been when he turned from play to work. But Mrs. Wilson washed them herself, and they looked as white as the whitest lamb. I will not attempt to describe the delight of his mother, the triumph of Willie, or the gratification of his father, who saw in this good promise of his boy's capacity.

And Willie did ask his father the question with Mrs. Wilson's answer to which he had not been satisfied—the question whether God worked. His father's answer, after he had sat pondering for a while in his chair, was something to this effect.

"Yes, Willie, it seems to me that God works more than anybody—for He works all night and all day and, if I remember rightly, Jesus tells us somewhere that He works all Sunday too. If He were to stop working, everything would stop being. The sun would stop shining, and the moon and stars; the corn would stop growing; there would be no apples or gooseberries; your eyes would stop seeing; your ears would stop hearing; your fingers couldn't move an inch; and, worst of all, your little heart would stop loving."

"No, Papa," cried Willie. "I shouldn't stop loving, I'm sure."

"Indeed you would, Willie."

"Not you and Mamma."

"Yes—you wouldn't love us any more than if you were asleep without dreaming."

"That would be dreadful."

"Yes, it would. So you see how good God is to us—to go on working, that we may be able to love each other."

"Then if God works like that all day long, it must be a fine thing to work," said Willie.

"You are right. It is a fine thing to work—the finest thing in the world, if it comes of love, as God's work does."

This conversation made Willie quite determined to learn to knit. If God worked, he would work too. And although the work he undertook was a very small work, it was like all God's great works; for every loop he made had a little love looped up in it, like an invisible, soft, downy lining to the stockings. And after those, he went on knitting a pair for his father, and learned to work with a needle as well, and to darn the stockings he had made.

CHAPTER THREE
The Blacksmith

Willie was now nine years old. His mother had been ill for some time—confined to her room, as she frequently was in the long cold winters. It was winter now, and one morning when all the air was dark with falling snow, Willie was standing by the parlor window looking out on it, and wondering whether the angels made it up in the sky. He thought it might be their sawdust, which, when they had too much, they shook down to get melted and put out of the way. Then Tibby came into the room very softly, looking, he thought, very strange.

"Willie, your mother wants you," she said, and Willie hastened upstairs to his mother's room. Dark as was the air outside, he was surprised to find how dark the room was. And what surprised him more was a curious noise—like a hedgehog, or some other little creature of the fields or woods. But he crept gently up to his mother's bed, saying, "Are you better this morning, Mamma?"

And she answered in a feeble sweet voice. "Yes, Willie, very much better. And, Willie, God has sent you a little sister."

"O-o-o-oh!" cried Willie. "A little sister! Did He make her Himself?"

"Yes. He made her Himself, and sent her to you last night."

"How busy He must have been lately!" said Willie. "Where is she? I *should* like to see her. Is she my very own sister?"

"Yes, your very own sister, Willie—to love and take care of always."

"Where is she?"

"Go and ask Nurse to let you see her."

Then Willie saw that there was another woman in the room, and something lying on her lap. He went up to her, and she folded back the corner of a blanket, and revealed a face no bigger than that of the big doll at the clergyman's house, but alive, quite alive—such a pretty little face! He stood staring at it for awhile.

"May I kiss her, Nurse?"

"Yes—gently—quite gently."

He kissed her, half afraid. Her cheek was softer and smoother than anything he had ever touched before. He sped back to his mother, too full of delight to speak. But she was not yet well enough to talk to him, and his father came in and led him downstairs again. Willie began once more to watch the snow, wondering now if it had anything to do with the baby's arrival.

In the afternoon, it was found that the lock of his mother's room not only would not catch easily, but made a noise that disturbed her. So while Willie watched, his father got a screwdriver and removed it, making as little noise as he could. Next he contrived a piece of string to keep the door shut, and as that would not hold it close enough, hung a shawl over it to keep the draft out.

As soon as he had finished, and the nurse had closed the door behind them, Dr. MacMichael set out to take the lock to the blacksmith, and allowed Willie to go with him. By the time they reached it, the snow was an inch deep on their shoulders, on Willie's cap, and on his father's hat. How red the glow of the smith's fire looked! It was a great cavern with a red heart in the midst of whiteness.

The smith was a great powerful man, with bare arms and blackened face. When they entered, he and two other men were making the axle of a wheel. They had a great lump of red-hot iron on the anvil, and were knocking a big hole through it—not boring it, but knocking it through with a big punch.* One of the men, with a pair of tongs-like pincers, held the punch steady in the hole, while the other two struck the head of it with alternate blows of mighty hammers called sledges. Each sledge took the strength of two brawny arms to heave high above the head with a great round swing over the shoulder, that it might come down with right good force, and drive the punch through four inches of glowing iron. All this Willie thought he could understand, for he knew that fire made the hardest metal soft.

But he couldn't at all understand this: every now and then when they stopped heaving their mighty sledges, the third man took the punch out of the hole, and the smith himself, whose name was Willet (and *will it* he did with a vengeance, when he had anything on the anvil before him), caught up his tongs in his hand, then picked up a little bit of black coal with the tongs and dropped it into the hole where the punch had been, where it took fire immediately and blazed up. Then in went the punch again, and again the huge hammering commenced, with such bangs and blows, that the smith was wise to have no floor for his smithy, for they would surely have knocked a hole in that, though they were not able to knock the anvil down halfway into the earth.

While this was going on, Dr. MacMichael, perceiving that the operation ought not to be interrupted any more than a surgical one, stood quite still waiting, and Willie stood also—absorbed in staring, and gradually creeping nearer and nearer to the anvil. There were no sparks flying about to make it dangerous to the eyes, as there would have been if they had been striking on the iron itself instead of the punch.

As soon as the punch was driven through, and the smith

had dropped his sledgehammer and begun to wipe his forehead, Willie spoke.

"Mr. Willet," he said, for he knew every man of any standing in the village by name and profession, "why did you put bits of coal into the hole you were making? I should have thought it would be in the way rather then help you."

"So it would, my little man," answered Willet, with no grim though grimy smile, "if it didn't take fire and keep getting out of the way all the time it kept up the heat. We depend on the heat for getting through, and it's much less trouble to drop a bit of coal or two in the hole, than to take up the big axle and lay it in the fire again, not to mention the time and the quantity of coal it would take to heat it up afresh."

"But such little bits of coal couldn't do much?" said Willie.

"They could do enough, and all that's less after that is saving," said the smith, who was one of those men who can not only do a thing right but give a reason for it. "You see, I was able to put the little bits just in the right place."

"I see! I see!" cried Willie. "I understand! But, Papa, do you think Mr. Willet is the proper person to ask to set your lock right?"

"I haven't a doubt of it," said Dr. MacMichael, taking it out of his coat pocket and unfolding the piece of paper in which he had wrapped it. "Why do you make a question of it?"

"Because look what great big huge things he does! How could those tremendous hammers set such a little thing as that right? They would knock it all to pieces. Don't you think you had better take it to the watchmaker?"

"If I did, Willie, do you know what you would say the moment you saw him at work?"

"No, Papa. What should I say?"

"You would say, 'Don't you think, Papa, you had better take it to the smith?'"

"But why should I say that?"

"Because, when you saw his tools beside this lock, you

would think the tools so small and the lock so huge, that nothing could be done between them. Yet I daresay the watchmaker could set the lock right if he chose to try. Don't you think so, Mr. Willet?"

"Not a doubt of it," answered the smith.

"Had we better go to him then?"

"Well," answered the smith, smiling, "I think perhaps he would ask you why you hadn't come to me. No doubt he could do it, but I've got better tools for the purpose. Let me look at the lock. I'm sure I shall be able to set it right."

"Not with that great big hammer, then," said Willie.

"No—I have smaller hammers than that. When do you want it, sir?"

"Could you manage to do it at once, and let me take it home, for there's a little baby there, just arrived?"

"You don't mean it!" said the smith, looking surprised. "I wish you joy, sir."

"And this is the lock of the room she's in," continued the doctor.

"And you're afraid of her getting out and flying off again!" said the smith. "I will do it at once. There isn't much wrong with it, I daresay. I hope Mrs. MacMichael is doing well, sir."

He took the lock, drew several screws from it, and then forced it open.

"It's nothing but the spring gone," he said, as he took out something and threw it away.

Then he took out several more pieces, and cleaned them all. Then he searched in a box till he found another spring, which he put in instead of the broken one, after snipping off a little bit with a pair of pincers. Then he put all the pieces in, put on its cover, gave a few taps with a tiny hammer, replaced the screws, and said, "Shall I come and put it on for you, sir?"

"No, no. I am up to that much," said Dr. MacMichael. "I can easily manage that. Come, Willie. I am much obliged to you for doing it at once. Goodnight."

Then out they went into the snowstorm again, Willie holding fast by his father's hand.

"This is good," said his father. "Your mother will have a better day all tomorrow, and perhaps a longer sleep tonight for it. You see how easy it is to be both useful and kind sometimes. The smith did more for your mother in those few minutes than ten doctors could have done. Think of his great black fingers making a little more sleep and rest and warmth for her—and all in those few minutes!"

"Suppose he couldn't have done it," said Willie. "Do you think the watchmaker could?"

"That I can't tell, but I don't think it likely. We should most probably have had to get a new one."

"Suppose you couldn't get a new one?"

"Then we should have to set our wits to work, and contrive some other way of fastening the door, so that Mamma shouldn't take cold by its being open, nor yet be disturbed by the noise of it."

"It would be so nice to be able to do everything!" said Willie.

"So it would, but nobody can, and it's just as well, for then we should not need so much help from each other, and would be too independent."

"Then shouldn't a body try to do as many things as he can?"

"Yes, for there's no fear of ever being able to do without other people, and you would be so often able to help them. Both the smith and the watchmaker could mend a lock, but neither of them could do without the other for all that."

When Willie went to bed, he lay awake a long time, thinking how, if the lock could not have been mended, and there had been no other to be had, he could have contrived to keep the door shut properly. In the morning, however, he told his father that he had not thought of any way that would do, for though he thought he could contrive to shut and open the door well enough, he could not think how a person outside might be able to do it. He thought the best way, if such a difficulty should occur, would be to take the lock off his door, and put it on Mamma's till a better one could be had. Of this suggestion his father, much to Willie's satisfaction, entirely approved.

CHAPTER FOUR
The Night Apprentice

Willie's mother grew better, and Willie's sister grew bigger. The nurse went away, and Willie and his mother and Tibby, with a little occasional assistance from the doctor, managed the baby among them. Considering that she had been yet only a short time at life's school, she behaved wonderfully well. She never cried except when she was in some trouble, and even then you could seldom have seen a tear on her face. She did all that was required of her, grew longer and broader and heavier, and was very fond of a lighted candle. The only fault she had was that she wouldn't give Willie quite so many smiles as he wanted. As to the view she took of affairs, she seemed for a long time to be on the whole very well satisfied with life and its gifts.

But when at last its troubles began to overtake her, she did not approve of them at all. The first thing she objected to was being weaned, which she evidently considered a very cruel and unnecessary experience. But her father said it must be, and her mother, believing him to know best, carried out his decree. Little Agnes endured it tolerably well in the daytime, but in the night she protested lustily—was indeed so outrageously indignant, that one evening the following conversation took place at the tea table, where Willie sat and heard it.

"Really, my dear," said Mrs. MacMichael, "I cannot have your rest disturbed in this way another night. You must go to Willie's room, and let me manage Agnes myself."

"Why shouldn't I take my share of the trouble?" objected her husband.

"Because you may be called up any moment, and have no more sleep till the next night, and it's not fair that what sleep your work does let you have should be so unnecessarily broken. It's not as if I couldn't manage without you."

"But Willie's bed is not big enough for both of us," he objected.

"Then Willie can come and sleep with me."

"But Willie wants his sleep as much as I do mine."

"There's no fear of him: he would sleep though all the babies in Priory Leas were crying in the room."

Would I really? thought Willie, feeling rather ashamed of himself.

"But who will get up and warm the milk and water for you?" pursued the father.

"Oh, I can manage that quite well."

"Couldn't I do that, Mamma?" said Willie very humbly, for he thought of what his mother had said about his sleeping powers.

"No, my pet," she answered, and he said no more.

"It seems to be a very clumsy necessity," said his father. "I have been thinking it over. To keep a fire in all night only to warm such a tiny drop of water as she wants, I must say, seems like using a steam engine to sweep up the crumbs. If you would just get a stone bottle, fill it with boiling water, wrap a piece of flannel about it, and lay it anywhere in the bed, it would be quite hot enough even in the morning to make the milk as warm as she ought to have it."

"If you will go to Willie's room, and let Willie come and sleep with me, I will try it," she said.

Dr. MacMichael consented, and Willie was filled with silent delight at the thought of sleeping next to his mother and the baby. And he resolved that he would try to get a share in the business of the night: why should his mother have too little sleep rather than himself? They might at least divide the too little between them! So he went to bed early, full of the thought of waking up as soon as Agnes should begin to cry, and finding out what he could do. Already he had begun to be useful in the daytime, and had twice put her to sleep when both his mother and Tibby had failed. And although he quite understood that in all probability he would not have succeeded if they hadn't tried first, yet it had been some relief to them, and they had confessed it.

But when he woke, there lay his mother and his sister both sound asleep; the sun was shining through the blind; he heard Tibby about the house; and, in short, it was time to get up.

At breakfast his father said to him, "Well, how did Agnes behave herself last night?"

"So well!" answered Willie. "She never cried once."

"O Willie!" said his mother, laughing. "She screamed for a whole hour, and was so hungry after it that she emptied her bottle without stopping once. You were sound asleep all the time, and never stirred."

Willie was so much ashamed of himself, although he wasn't in the least to blame, that he could hardly keep from crying. He did not say another word, except when he was spoken to, all through breakfast, and his father and mother were puzzled to think what could be the matter with him. He went about the greater part of the morning moodily thinking, and then went for advice to Mrs. Wilson. She suggested several things, none of which, however, seemed to him likely to succeed.

"If I could only go to bed after Mamma was asleep," he said, "I could tie a string to my hair, and then slip a loop at the other end over Mamma's wrist, so that when she sat up to attend to Agnes, she would pull my hair and wake me up. Wouldn't she wonder what it was when she felt it pulling her?"

He had to go home without any help from Mrs. Wilson. All the way he kept thinking. "Mamma won't wake me, and Agnes can't, and the worst of it is that everybody else will be just as fast asleep as I shall be. Let me see—who *is* there that's awake all night? There's the cat: I think she is, but then she wouldn't know when to wake me, and even if I could teach her to wake me the moment Agnes cried, I don't think she would be a nice one to do it, for if I didn't come awake with a pat of her velvety pincushions, she might turn out the points of the pins in them and scratch me awake. There's the clock—it's always awake, but it can't tell you the time till you go and ask it. I think it might be made to wind up a string that should pull me when the right time came, but I don't think I could teach it. And the pull might stop the clock, and what would Papa say then? They tell me the owls are up all night, but they're no good, I'm certain. I don't see what I *am* to do. I wonder if God would wake me if I were to ask Him?"

Willie fell asleep with his head and heart full so of desire to wake in the middle of the night, he did wake up suddenly, and there was little Agnes screaming with all her might. He sat up in bed instantly.

"What's the matter, Willie?" said his mother. "Lie down and go to sleep."

"Baby's crying," said Willie.

"Never you mind. I'll manage her."

"Do you know, Mamma, I think I was waked up just in time to help you. I'll take her from you, and perhaps she will take her drink from me."

"Nonsense, Willie. Lie down, my pet."

"But I've been thinking about it, Mamma. Do you remember, yesterday, Agnes would not take her bottle from you, and screamed and screamed, but when Tibby took her, she gave in and drank it all? Perhaps she would do the same with me."

As he spoke he slipped out of bed, and held out his arms to take the baby. A little light was already coming in through the blind, for it was summer. He heard a cow lowing in the fields at the back of the house, and he wondered whether her own baby had wakened her. The next moment he had little Agnes in his arms.

So Willie walked about the room with Agnes till his mother had got her bottle filled with nice warm milk and water and just a little sugar. When she gave it to him, he sat down with the baby on his knees and, to his great delight and the satisfaction of his mother, she stopped crying, and began to drink the milk and water.

"Why, you're a born nurse, Willie!" said his mother.

But the moment the baby heard her mother's voice, she forsook the bottle, and began to scream, wanting to go to her.

"O Mamma! You mustn't speak, please—for of course she likes you better than the bottle, and when you speak that reminds her of you. It was just the same with Tibby yesterday. Or if you must speak, speak with some other sound, and not in your own soft, sweet way."

A few moments after, Willie was so startled by a gruff voice in the room that he nearly dropped the bottle, but it was only his mother following his directions. The plan was quite successful, for the baby had not a suspicion that the voice was her mother's; she paid no heed to it, and attended only to her bottle.

Dr. MacMichael, who had been out in the country, was creeping up the stairs to his room, fearful of disturbing his wife, when what should he hear but a man's voice! And what should he think but that robbers had broken in! Of course he went to his wife's room first. There he heard the voice plainly enough through the door, but when he opened it he could see no one except Willie feeding the baby on an ottoman at the foot of the bed. When his wife had explained what and why it was, they both laughed heartily over Willie's suggestion for leaving the imagination of little Agnes in repose, and henceforth he was installed as night nurse, so long as the process of weaning should last—and very proud of his promotion he was. He slept as sound as ever, for he had no anxiety about waking; his mother always woke him the instant Agnes began to cry.

"Willie!" she would say, "Willie! Here's your baby wanting you."

And up Willie would start, sometimes before he was able to open his eyes. And once he jumped out of bed crying, "Where is she, Mamma! I've lost her!" for he had been dreaming about her.

His mother always let him have a long sleep in the morning, to make up for being disturbed in the night.

Agnes soon grew reconciled to the bottle, and then Willie slept in peace.

CHAPTER FIVE

The Shoemaker's Business

Time passed, and Willie grew. Now growing is far from meaning only that you get bigger and stronger; it means that you become able both to understand and to wonder at more of the things about you.

There are people who the more they understand, wonder the less: these are not growing straight, but are growing crooked. There are two ways of growing: growing up or growing down, and if you are doing both at once, then you are growing crooked. There are people who are growing up in understanding, but down in goodness. It is a beautiful fact, however, that you can't grow up in goodness and down in understanding; while the great probability is, that, if you are not growing better, you will by and by begin to grow stupid. Those who are growing the right way, the more they understand, the more they wonder; and the more they learn to do, the more they want to do. Willie was a boy of this kind.

Agnes grew as well, and the more Willie grew capable of helping her, the more he found Agnes required of him. It was a long time, however, before he knew how much he was obliged to Agnes for requiring so much of him.

When she was capable of playing with a doll, of course a doll was given her—not a new one just bought, but a most respectable old doll, a big one that had been her mother's when she was a little girl. Her mother made some new clothes for it now, and Tibby made a cloak and bonnet for her to wear when she went out-of-doors. But it struck Willie that the doll's shoes, which were only of cloth, were very unfit for walking. He thought that in a doctor's family, it was something quite amazing that while the head and shoulders were properly looked after, the feet should remain utterly neglected. It was clear that must be his part in the affair. It could not be anybody else's, for in that case someone else would have attended to it.

Willie knew almost everybody in the village, and everybody knew him. He was a favorite—first of all, because his father was much loved and trusted; next, because his mother spoke as kindly to her husband's poor patients as to the richer ones; and last, because he himself spoke to everybody with proper respect. Some of the people, of course, he knew better than others. Of these Mrs. Wilson was one. But in the house she lived in, there were other poor people. In the room opposite to hers, on the ground floor, lived and worked Mr. MacAllaster, a shoemaker—a man who had neither wife nor child, nor, so far as people knew, any near relative at all. He was far from being in good health, and although he worked from morning to night, had a constant pain in his back, which was rather crooked, with a little hump on it. His temper was not always of the best, but I wonder what watch or steam engine would go as well as he did with such a twist in *its* back.

His stool was low, and he sat in a leather covered hole in it, perhaps for the sake of the softness and spring of the leather. His head and body were bent forward over his lapstone or his last, and his right hand with the quick broadheaded hammer hammered up and down on a piece of sole leather. Sometimes both his hands would meet as if for a little friendly chat about something small, and then suddenly start asunder as if in astonished anger, with a portentous hiss. You might have taken him for an automaton moved by springs, and imitating human actions in a very wonderful manner—so regular and machinelike were his motions, and so little did he seem to think about what he was doing. His hands were so used to their work, and had been so well taught by his head, that they could have nearly made a pair of shoes by themselves.

The shoemaking trade is one that admits a great deal of thought, and shoemakers have distinguished themselves both in poetry and in prose. If Hector MacAllaster had done so in neither, he could yet think, and that is what some people who write both poetry and prose cannot do. But it is infinitely more important to be able to think well than merely to write ever so well—and to think well is what everybody ought to be or to become able to do.

Hector had odd ways of looking at things. Ever since the illness from which he had risen with a weak spine, an ever-working brain, and a quiet heart, he had shown himself not merely a good sort of man, for such he had always been, but a religious man; not by saying much, for he was modest even to shyness with grown people, but by the solemnity of his look when a great word was spoken, by his unblamable behavior, and by the readiness with which he would lend or give his small earnings to his poor neighbors.

The only thing of which anybody could complain was his temper—but it showed itself only occasionally, and almost everybody made excuses for it because of Hector's bodily ailments. He gave it no quarter himself, however. He said once to the clergyman, to whom he had been lamenting the trouble he had with it, and who had sought to comfort him by saying that it was caused by the weakness of his health. "No, sir—excuse me; nobody knows how much I am indebted to my crooked back. If it weren't for that I might have a bad temper and never know it. But that drives it out of its hole, and when I see the ugly head of it I know it's there, and try once more to starve it to death. But it's such a creature to burrow! When I think I've built it in all round, out comes its head again at a place where I never looked to see it, and it's all to do over again!" The shoemaker thought after his own fashion, which is the way everybody who can think does think.

When Willie entered his room this day, Hector greeted him with a very friendly nod. Not only was he fond of children, but he had a special favor for Willie, chiefly because he considered himself greatly indebted to him for something he had said to Mrs. Wilson, and which had given him a good deal to think about. For Mrs. Wilson often had a chat with Hector, and then she would not infrequently talk about Willie, of whose friendship she was quite proud. She had told Hector of the strange question Willie had put to her as to whether God worked, and the shoemaker, thinking it over, had come to the same conclusion as Willie's father, and it had been a great comfort and help to him.

"What can I do for you today, Willie? You look as if you wanted something."

"I want you to teach me to make shoes," answered Willie.

"Do you think that would be prudent of me? Don't you see, if I were to teach you to make shoes, people would be coming to you to make their shoes for them, and what would become of me then?"

"But I only want to make shoes for Aggy's doll. She oughtn't to go without shoes in this weather, you know."

"Certainly not. Well, if you will bring me the doll I will take her measure and make her a pair."

"But I don't think Papa could afford to pay for shoes for a doll as well as for all of us. You see, though it would be better, it's not necessary that a doll have strong shoes. She should have shoes good enough for indoors, but she needn't walk in the wet. Don't you think so yourself, Hector?"

"But," returned Hector, "I shall be happy to make Agnes a present of a pair of shoes for her doll. I shouldn't think of charging your papa for that. He is far too good a man to be made to pay for everything."

"But," objected Willie, "to let you make them for nothing would be as bad as to make Papa pay for them when they aren't necessary. Please, you must let *me* make them for Aggy. Besides, she's not old enough yet even to say *thank you* for them."

"Then she won't be old enough to say *thank you* to you either," said Hector, who, all this time, had been losing no moment from his work, but was stitching away, with a bore and a twiddle and a hiss at the sole of a huge boot.

"Ah! But she's my own, so it doesn't matter!"

This set Hector thinking. Instead of replying, however, he laid down his boot, rose, and first taking from a shelf a whole skin of calf leather, and next a low chair from a corner of the room, he set the latter near his own seat opposite the window.

"Sit down there, then, Willie," he said, adding, as he handed him the calfskin, "there's your leather, and my tools are at your service. Make your shoes, and welcome. I shall be glad of your company." He sat down again and began stitching away.

Willie took the calfskin on his lap, somewhat bewildered. If he had been asked to cut out a pair of seven-league boots for an ogre, there would have seemed to his eyes enough of leather for them in that one skin. But however was he to find two pieces small enough for a doll's shoes in such an ocean of leather? He began to turn it round and round, looking at it all along the edge, while Hector was casting sidelong glances at him in the midst of his busyness.

Willie, although he had never yet considered how shoes are made, had seen at once that nothing could be done until he had command of a manageable bit of leather. He found too much to be only a shade better than too little, and he saw it wouldn't be wise to cut a piece out just anywhere, for that might spoil what would serve for a large pair of shoes or even boots. Therefore he kept turning the skin round until he came to a small projecting piece. This he contemplated for some time, trying to recall the size of Dolly's feet, and to make up his mind whether it would not be large enough for one or even for both shoes.

A smile of satisfaction passed over Hector's face. "That's it!" he said. "I think you'll do. That's the first thing—to consider your stuff, and see how much you can make of it. Waste is a thing that no good shoemaker ever yet could endure. It's bad in itself, and so unworkmanlike! Yes, I think that corner will do. Shall I cut it off for you?"

"No, thank you—not yet, please. I think I must go and look at her feet, for I can't recollect *quite* how big they are. I'll just run home and look."

"Do you think you will be able to carry the exact size in your head, and bring it back with you?"

"Yes, I think I shall."

"I don't. I never could trust myself so far as that. You might be pretty near it one way and all wrong another, for you have to consider length and breadth and roundabout. I will tell you the best way for *you* to do. Set the doll standing on a bit of paper, and draw a pencil all round her foot with the point close to it on the paper. Both feet will be better, for it would be a mistake to suppose they were the same size. That will give you the size of the sole. Then take a strip of paper and see how long a piece it takes to go round the thickest part of the foot, and cut it off to that length. That will be sufficient measurement for a doll's shoe, for even if it should not fit exactly, she won't mind either being pinched a little or having to walk a little loose."

Willie got up at once to go and do as Hector had told him, but Hector was not willing to part with his company so soon. Therefore he said, "But don't you think, Willie, before you set about it, you had better see how I do? It would be a pity to spend your labor in finding out for yourself what shoemakers have known for hundreds of years, and which you could learn so easily by letting me show you."

"Thank you," said Willie, sitting down again. "I should like that very much. I know what you are doing now—fastening on the sole of a boot."

"Yes. Do you see how it's done?"

"I'm not sure. Of course, I see you are sewing the one to the other. I've often wondered how you could manage with small shoes like mine to get in your hand to pull the needle through. But I see you don't use a needle, and you are sewing it all on the outside of the boot, and don't put your hand inside at all."

"All round the edge of the upper, as we call it, I have sewn on a strong narrow strip, so that one edge of the strip sticks out all round, while the other is inside. To the edge that sticks out I sew on the sole, drawing my threads so tight that when I pare the edges off smooth, it will look like one piece, and puzzle anybody who did not know how it was done."

"But how do you get your thread so sharp and stiff as to go through the holes you make?"

"Look here."

"I see!" cried Willie. "There is a long bit of something else, not thread, upon it. What is it? It looks like a hair, only thicker, and it is so sharp at the point!"

"It is a bristle of a hog's back. I don't know what a shoemaker would do without them. Look, here's a little bunch of them."

"That's a very clever use to put them to," said Willie. "Do you go and pluck them out of the pigs?"

"No, we buy them at the shop. We want a good many, for they wear out. They get too soft, and though they don't break right off, they double up in places, so that they won't go through."

"How do you fasten them to the thread?"

"Look here," said Hector. He took several strands of thread, and drew them through and through a piece of cobbler's wax, then took a bristle and put it in at the end cunningly, and then rolled threads and all over and over between his hand and his leather apron, till it seemed like a single dark-colored cord. "There, you see, is my needle and thread all in one."

"And what is the good of rubbing it so much with the cobbler's wax?"

"There are several good reasons for doing that. In the first place, it makes all the threads into one by sticking them together. Next, it would be worn out before I had drawn it many times through but for the wax, which keeps the rubbing from wearing it. The wax also protects it afterward, and keeps the wet from rotting it. The waxed thread fills the hole better too, and it sticks so that the last stitch doesn't slacken before the next comes, but holds tight. The two pieces are thus sewn so close together that they are like one piece, as you will see when I pare the joined edges."

More professional talk followed. But the shoemaker cared for other things besides shoemaking, and after a while he happened to make a remark which led to a question from Willie.

"Do you understand astronomy, Hector?"

"No. It's not my business, you see, Willie."

"But you've just been telling me so much about the moon, and the way she keeps turning her face always to us—in the politest manner, as you said!"

"I got it all out of an astronomy book. I don't understand it. I don't know why she does so. I know a few things that are not my business, just as you know a little about shoemaking, that not being your business. But I don't understand them for all that."

"Whose business is astronomy, then?"

"Well," answered Hector, a little puzzled, "I don't see how

it can well be anybody's business but God's, for I'm sure no one else can lay a hand to it."

"And what's your business, Hector?" asked Willie, in a half-absent mood. If this was a stupid question, it was not because Willie was stupid. People sometimes appear stupid because they have more things to think about than they can well manage, while those who think only about one or two things may appear clever when those one or two things are talked about.

"What is my business, Willie? Why, to keep people out of the dirt, of course, by making and mending their shoes. The astronomer, now, when he goes out to look at the stars through his telescope, might get his death of cold if his shoemaker did not know his business. Of the general business, it's a part God keeps to Himself to see that the stars go all right, and that the sun rises and sets at the proper times. But I don't understand about astronomy, because it's not my business. I'm set to keep folk's feet off the cold and wet earth, and stones and broken glass—for however much a man may be an astronomer and look up at the sky, he must touch the earth with some part of him, and generally does so with his feet."

"And God sets you to do it, Hector?"

"Yes. It's the way He looks after people's feet. He's got to look after everything, you know, or everything would go wrong. So He gives me the leather and the tools and the hands—and I must say the head, for it wants no little head to make a *good* shoe to measure—as if He said to me, 'There! You make shoes, while I keep the stars right.' Isn't it a fine thing to have a hand in the general business?" And Hector looked up with shining eyes in the face of the little boy.

"I think it's a fine thing to have to make nice new shoes," said Willie, "but I don't think I should like to mend them when they are soppy and muddy and out of shape."

"If you would take your share in the general business, you mustn't be particular. It won't do to be above your business—or *below* it. There's those boots in the corner now. They belong to your papa. And they come next. Don't you think it's an honor to keep the feet of such a good man dry and warm as he goes about from morning to night comforting people? Don't you think it's an honor to mend boots for *him,* even if they should be dirty?"

"Oh, yes! For Papa!" said Willie, as if his papa must be an exception to any rule.

"Well," resumed Hector, "look at these great lace-boots. I shall have to fill their soles full of hobnails presently. They belong to the best plowman in the parish —John Turnbull. Don't you think it's an honor to mend boots for a man who makes the best bed for the corn to die in?"

"I thought it was to grow in," said Willie.

"All the same," returned Hector. "When it dies, it grows— and not till then, as you will read in the New Testament. Isn't it an honor, I say, to mend boots for John Turnbull?"

"Oh, yes—for John Turnbull! I know John," said Willie, as if it made any difference to his merit whether Willie knew him or not.

"And there," Hector went on, "lies a pair of slippers that want patching. They belong to William Webster, the weaver round the corner. But isn't it an honor to patch slippers for a man who keeps his neighbors in fine linen all the days of their lives?"

"Yes, yes. I know William. It must be nice to do anything for William Webster."

"Suppose you didn't know him, would that make any difference?"

"No," said Willie, after thinking a little. "Other people would know him if I didn't."

"Yes, and if nobody knew him, God would know him, and anybody God has thought worth making, it's an honor to do anything for. Believe me, Willie, to have to keep people's feet dry and warm is a very important appointment."

"Your own shoes aren't very good, Hector," said Willie, who had been glancing at his companion's feet. "Isn't it an honor to make shoes for yourself?"

"There can't be much honor in doing anything for yourself," replied Hector, "so far as I can see. I confess my shoes are hardly decent, but then I can make myself a pair anytime—and I've been thinking I would for the last three months, as soon as a slack time came. But I've been far too busy as yet, and, as I don't go out much till after it's dusk, nobody sees them."

"But what if you should get your feet wet and catch cold?"

"Ah! That might be the death of me!" said Hector. "I really must make myself a pair. Well now—let me see—as soon as I have mended those two pairs tomorrow, I will begin. And I'll tell you what," he added, after a thoughtful pause, "if you'll come to me the day after tomorrow, I will take that skin and cut out a pair of shoes for myself, and you shall see how I do it, and everything about the making of them. You shall do some part of them yourself, and that shall be your first lesson in shoemaking."

"But Dolly's shoes!" suggested Willie.

"Dolly can wait a bit. She won't take *her* death of cold from wet feet. And let me tell you it is harder to make a small pair well than a large pair. You will do Dolly's ever so much better after you know how to make a pair for me."

CHAPTER SIX

Willie Learns to Read

The next day Willie's thoughts, having nothing particular to engage them, kept brooding over two things. These two things came together all at once, and a resolution was the consequence.

First, Hector had shown considerable surprise when he found that Willie could not read. Now Willie was not in the least ashamed that he could not read: why should he be? It was nowhere written in the catechism he had learned that it was his duty to learn to read; and if the catechism had merely forgotten to mention it, his father and mother would have told him. Neither was it a duty he ought to have known of himself—for then he would have known it. So why should he be ashamed?

People are often ashamed of what they need not be ashamed of. Again, they are often not at all ashamed of what they ought to be ashamed of, and will turn up their faces to the sun when they ought to hide them in the dust. If, for instance, Willie had ever put on a sulky face when his mother asked him to hold the baby for her, that would have been a thing of shame which the skin of his face might well try to burn off. But not to be able to read before he had ever been made to think about it was not at all a thing to be ashamed of: it would have been more of a shame to be ashamed. Now that it had been put into his head to think what a good thing reading was, all this would no longer apply. It was a very different thing now.

The other subject which occupied his thought was that everybody was so kind to him—so ready to do things for him—and, what was of far more consequence, to teach him to do them himself; while he, so far as he could think, did nothing for anybody! That could not be right; it *could* not be—for it was not reasonable. Not to mention his father and mother, there was Mrs. Wilson, who had taught him to knit, and even given him a few lessons in spinning, though that had not come to much; and here was Hector MacAllaster going to teach him to make shoes—and he could not think of one thing that he was capable of doing in return!

All at once it struck Willie that Hector had said, with some regret in his voice, that though he had plenty of time to think, he had very little time to read—and that he could see well enough by candlelight to work at his trade, but he could not see well enough to read. What a fine thing it would be to learn to read to Hector! It would be such fun to surprise him too, by all at once reading something to him!

The moment Willie saw that he ought to learn to read, he ran to his mother to ask her to teach him. She was delighted, for she had begun to be a little doubtful whether his father's plan of leaving him alone till he wanted to learn was the right one. But at that precise moment she was too busy with something that must be done for his father to lay it down and begin teaching him his letters. Willie was so eager to learn, however, that he could not rest without doing something toward it. He thought a little, then ran and got Dr. Watts' hymns for children. He knew "How doth the little busy bee" so well as to be able to repeat it without a mistake, for his mother had taught it to him, and he had understood it. He was not like a child of five, taught to repeat by rote lines which could give him no notions but mistaken ones. Besides, he had a good knowledge of words, and could use them well in talk, although he could not read—and it is a great thing if a child can talk well before he begins to read.

Willie opened the little book at the Busy Bee, and already knowing enough to be able to divide the words one from the other, he said to himself, "The first word must be *How*. There it is, with a gap between it and the next word. I will look and see if I can find another *How* anywhere."

He looked a long time before he found one, for the capital *H* was in the way. Of course there were a good many *hows*, but not many with a big *H*, and Willie didn't know that the little *h* was just as good for the mere word. Then he looked for *doth*, and he found several. Of *the* he found as great a swarm as if they had been busy bees themselves. *Busy* was scarce; I am not sure whether he found it at all, but he looked until he was pretty sure he should know it again when he saw it. After he had gone over in this way every word of the first verse, he tried himself, by putting his finger at random here and there upon it, and seeing whether he could tell the word it happened to touch. Sometimes he could, and sometimes he couldn't. However, before the day was over, he knew at least a dozen words perfectly well at sight.

This was a great step in the direction of reading, for it would be easy for Willie afterward to break up these words into letters.

It took him two days more—for during part of each he was learning to make shoes—to learn to know anywhere every word he had found in that hymn. Next he took a hymn he had not learned, and applied to his mother when he came to a word he did not know. As soon as she told him one, he hunted about until he found more specimens of the same, and so went on until he had quite fixed it in his mind.

Then he began to compare words that were like each other, and by discovering where they looked the same, and where they looked different, he learned something of the sounds of the letters. For instance, in comparing *the* and *these,* although the one sound of the two letters, *t* and *h,* puzzled him, and likewise the silent *e,* he conjectured that the *s* must stand for the hissing sound; and when he looked at other words which had that sound, and perceived an *s* in every one of them, then he was sure of it. His mother had no idea how fast he was learning, and when about a fortnight after he had begun, she was able to take him in hand, she found, to her astonishment, that he could read a great many words, but that he had not the least notion of what spelling meant.

"Isn't that a *b*?" she said, wishing to help him to find out a certain word for himself.

"I don't know," answered Willie. "It's not the busy bee," he added, laughing. "I should know him! It must be the lazy one, I suppose."

"Don't you know your letters?" asked his mother.

"No, Mamma. Which are they? Are the rest yours and Papa's?"

"Oh, you silly dear!" she said.

"Of course I am!" he returned. "Very silly! How could any of them be mine before I know the names of them! When I know them all, then they'll all be mine, I suppose, and everybody else's who knows them. So that's Mr. B, is it?"

"Yes, and that's C," said his mother.

"I'm glad to see you, Mr. C," said Willie, merrily, nodding to the letter. "We shall know each other when we meet again. I suppose this is D, Mamma. How d'e do, Mr. D? And what's this one with its mouth open, and half its tongue cut off?"

His mother told him it was E.

"Then this one, with no foot to stand on, is Fee, I suppose."

His mother laughed—but whoever gave it the name it has, would have done better to call it Fee, as Willie did. It would be much better also to call H Hee, and W Wee, and Y Yee, and Z Zee, as Willie called them. But it was easy enough for him to learn their names after he knew so much of what they could *do*.

He had begun with verse, and not dry syllables and stupid sentences. The music of the verse repaid him at once for the trouble of making it out—even before he got the meaning, while the necessity of making each line go right, and the rhymes too, helped him occasionally with the pronunciation of a word.

The farther he progressed, the faster he progressed, and before six weeks were over, Willie could read anything he was able to understand pretty well at sight.

By this time, also, he understood all the particulars as to how a shoe is made, and had indeed done a few stitches himself, a good deal of hammering both of leather and of hobnails, and a little patching, at which the smallness of his hands was an advantage.

One day he said to the shoemaker, "Shall I read a little poem to you, Hector?"

"You told me you couldn't read, Willie."

"I can now, though."

"Do then," said Hector.

Looking for but a small result in such a short time, Hector was considerably astonished to find how well the boy could read; for Willie not merely gave the words correctly, but the sentences, which is far more difficult—that is, he read so that Hector could understand what the writer meant. It is a great thing to read well. Few can. Whoever reads aloud and does not read well is a sort of deceiver, for he pretends to introduce one person to another, while he misrepresents him.

In later life, Willie continued to pay a good deal of attention not merely to reading for its own sake, but to reading for the sake of other people, that is, to reading aloud. In the course of his own reading, as often as he came to any verse that he liked very much, he always read it aloud in order to teach himself how it ought to be read. He did his best: first, to make it sound true—that is, to read it according to the sense—and next, to make it sound beautiful—that is, to read it according to the measure of the verse and the melody of the words.

He began coming to Hector at a certain time every day, to read to him for an hour and a half.

CHAPTER SEVEN
The Carpenter's Apprentice

When Willie's father found that he had learned to read, then he judged it good for him to go to school. Willie was very much pleased. His mother said she would make him a bag to carry his books in, but Willie said there was no occasion to trouble herself, for, if she would give him the stuff, he would make it. So she got him a nice bit of green baize,* and in the afternoon he made his bag—no gobble-stitch* work, but good honest backstitching. He passed the string through with a bodkin,* fixed it in the middle, tied the two ends, and carried the bag to his mother, who pronounced it nearly as well made as if she had done it herself.

At school he found it more and more plain what a good thing it is that we haven't to find out everything for ourselves from the beginning—that people gather into books what they and all who went before them have learned, so that we come into their property, as it were, and have only to begin our discoveries from where they leave off. In geography, for instance, what a number of voyages and journeys have had to be made, and books to record them written; then what a number of these books had to be read, and the facts gathered out of them, before a single map could be drawn, not to say a geography book printed! But now Willie could learn a multitude of things about the various countries, their peoples and animals and plants, their mountains and rivers and lakes and cities, without having set his foot beyond the parish in which he was born.

When he went to school, his father made him a present of a pocketknife. He had had one before, but not a very good one—and this, with three very sharp blades, was a wonderful treasure. His father also bought him a nice new slate.*

Now there was another handy boy at school, a couple of years older than Willie, whose father was a carpenter. He had cut on the frame of his slate, not his initials only, but his whole name and address: Alexander Spelman, Priory Lane. Willie thought how nice it would be with his new knife also to cut his name on his slate—only he would rather find a different way of doing it. What if, instead of sinking the letters in the frame, he made them stand up from the frame by cutting away to some depth all round them? There was not much originality in this, for it was only reversing what Spelman had done, but it was more difficult, and would, he thought, be prettier.

The boys at school couldn't imagine what Willie meant to do when they saw him draw first a D and then an O on the frame. But when they saw a C and T follow, they thought what a conceited little prig Willie was!

"Do you think you're a doctor because your father is, you little ape?" they said.

"No, no," answered Willie, laughing heartily, but thinking, as he went on with his work, that he might be some day.

When the drawing of the letters was finished, there stood, all round the slate, "Doctor MacMichael's Willie, The Ruins, Priory Leas."

Then out came his knife. But it was a long job, for Willie was not one of those slovenly boys that scamp their work. Such boys are nothing but soft, pulpy creatures, who, when they grow to be men, will be too soft for any of the hard work of the world. The carving, when finished, gave much satisfaction—first to Willie himself, because it was finished; next, to Alexander Spelman, because, being a generous-minded boy, he admired Willie's new and superior work;

third, to Dr. and Mrs. MacMichael, because they saw in it, not the boy's faculty merely, but his love to his father as well—for the recognition of a right over us is one of the sweetest forms love can take. "I am yours" is the best and greatest thing one can say, if to the right person.

It led to a strong friendship between him and Spelman, and to his going often to the workshop of the elder Spelman, the carpenter.

Mr. Spelman was a solemn, long-faced, and long-legged man, with reddish hair and pale complexion, who seldom or never smiled. At the bench he always looked as if he were standing on a stool, because he stooped so immoderately. He looked sickly, though he was in perfect health; he was only oppressed with the cares of his family, and the sickness of his invalid wife, who had more children than her husband thought she could manage, or he well provide for. But if he had thought less about it he would have got on better. He worked hard, but little fancied how many fewer strokes of his plane he made in an hour just because he was brooding over his difficulties, and imagining what would be the consequences if this or that misfortune were to befall him—of which he himself sought and secured the shadow beforehand, to darken and hinder the labor which might prevent its arrival. But he was a good man nevertheless, for his greatest bugbear* was debt. If he could only pay off every penny he owed in the world, and if only his wife were so far better as to enjoy life a little, he would, he thought, be perfectly happy. His wife, however, was tolerably happy, notwithstanding her weak health, and certainly enjoyed life a good deal—far more at least than her husband was able to believe.

Dr. MacMichael was very kind and attentive to Mrs. Spelman—though, as the carpenter himself said, he hadn't seen the color of *his* money for years. But the doctor knew that Spelman was a hard-working man, and would rather have given him a little money than have pressed him for a penny. He told Spelman one day, when that man was lamenting that he couldn't pay the doctor even *yet,* that he was only too glad to do anything in the least little bit like what the Saviour did when He was in the world—"a carpenter like you, Spelman—think of that," added the doctor.

So Spelman was as full of gratitude as he could hold. Except Hector MacAllaster, the doctor was almost his only creditor. Medicine and shoes were his chief trials: he kept on paying for the latter, but the debt for the former went on accumulating.

Hence, when Willie began to haunt his shop, though he had hardly a single smile to give the little fellow, he was more than pleased. He gave Willie odds and ends of wood; lent him whatever tools he wanted except the adze*—that he would not let him touch; would drop him a hint now and then as to the use of them; would any moment stop his own work to attend to a difficulty the boy found himself in; and, in short, paid him far more attention than he would have thought required of him if Willie had been his apprentice.

From the moment he entered the workshop, Willie could hardly keep his hands off the tools. The very shape of them, as they lay on the bench or hung on the wall, seemed to say over and over, "Come, use us." They looked waiting and hungry for work. They wanted stuff to shape and fashion into things, and join into other things. They wanted to make bigger tools than themselves—for plowing the earth, for carrying the harvest, or for some one or other of 10,000 services to be rendered in the house or in the fields. Willie could see none of them—the gouge, the chisel, the plane, the auger, the spokeshave, the hammer, or the humble bradawl*—without longing to send his life into theirs, and set them doing in the world.

At that time young Spelman was busy making a saltbox for his mother out of the sound bits of an old oak floor which his father had taken up because it was dry-rotted. It was hard wood to work, but Willie bore a hand in planing the pieces, and was initiated into the mysteries of dovetailing and gluing. Before the lid was put on by the hinges, he carved the initials of the carpenter and his wife in relief upon it, and many years after they used to show his work.

But the first thing he set about making for himself was a waterwheel. If he had been a seaside boy, his first job would have been a boat; if he had lived in a flat country, it would very likely have been a windmill; but the most noticeable thing in that neighborhood was a mill for grinding corn driven by a waterwheel.

When Willie was a tiny boy, he had gone once with Farmer Thomson's man and a load of corn to the mill. The miller had taken him all over it. Willie saw the corn go in by the hopper into the trough which was the real hopper, for it kept constantly hopping to shake the corn down through a hole in the middle of the upper stone, which went round and round against the lower, so that between them they ground the corn to meal. In the story beneath, he saw the meal pouring, a solid stream like an avalanche, from a wooden spout. But the best of it all was the wheel outside, and the busy rush of the water that made it go. So Willie would now make a waterwheel.

The carpenter had given him a short lecture on the different kinds of waterwheels, and Willie decided on an under-shot. With Sandy Spelman's help he constructed its nave of mahogany, its spokes of birch, its floats of deal, and its axle of stout iron wire, which was to run in gudgeon blocks* of well-oiled hardwood. These blocks were fixed in a frame so that, with the help of a few stones to support it, the wheel might be set going in any small stream.

There were many tiny brooks running into the river, and they fixed upon one of them which issued from the rising ground at the back of the village. Just where it began to run merrily down the hill, they constructed in its channel a stone bed for the waterwheel—not by any means for it to go to sleep in!

It worked delightfully, but after only a few days, Willie got tired of it—and small blame to him, for it was of no earthly use beyond amusement, and that which can only amuse can never amuse long. I think the reason children get tired of their toys so soon is that it is against human nature to be really interested in what is of no use. If you say that a beautiful thing is always interesting, then it must be said that a beautiful thing is of the highest use. Is not a diamond that flashes all its colors into the heart of a poet as useful as the diamond with which the glazier divides the sheets of glass into panes for our windows? Willie grew tired of his waterwheel because it went round and round, and did nothing but go round. It drove no machinery, ground no grain of corn—"Did nothing for *nobody*," Willie said emphatically. So he carried it home, and put it away in a certain part of the ruins where he kept odds and ends of things that might be of use someday.

Dr. MacMichael was so devoted to his profession that he desired nothing better for Willie than that he too should be a medical man, and he was more than pleased to find how well Willie's hands were able to carry out his contrivances; he judged it impossible for a country doctor to have too much mechanical faculty. The exercise of such a skill alone might secure the instant relief of a patient, and be the saving of him. But, more than this, he believed that nothing tended so much to develop common sense—the most precious of faculties—as the doing of things with the hands. Hence he not only encouraged Willie in everything he understood, but, considering the five hours of school quite sufficient for study of that sort, requested the master not to give him any lessons to do at home. So Willie worked hard during school, and after it had plenty of time to spend in carpentry. He soon came to use all the common bench tools with ease, and Spelman was proud of his apprentice, as he called him—so much so, that the burden of his debt grew much lighter upon his shoulders.

For twelve months his chief employment lay in the workshop of the carpenter, but Willie did not forget his older friend, Hector MacAllaster. Neither did he give up shoemaking, for he often did a little work for Hector, who had made him a leather apron, and cut him out bits of stout leather to protect his hands from the thread when he was sewing. Every half-holiday Willie read to Hector for a couple of hours, chiefly, for some time, from an astronomy book. Neither of them understood all he read, but both understood much, and Hector could explain some of the things that puzzled Willie. And when he found that everything went on in such order, above and below and all about him, Willie began to see that even a thing well done was worth a good deal more when done at the right moment or within the set time, and that the heavens themselves were like a great clock, ordering the time for everything.

CHAPTER EIGHT

Buried Treasure

Willie had been reading to Hector from Sir Walter Scott's
Antiquary, which describes digging for treasure in ruins not
unlike those of the Priory, only grander. It was of little
consequence to Willie that no treasure had been found
there, for the propriety of digging remained the same. In a
certain chamber in the priory ruins he had often fancied
that a hollow sound, when he stamped hard, indicated an
empty space underneath. A portion of the vaulted roof had
been broken in, and the floor was heaped up with fallen
stones and rubbish.

One Wednesday afternoon, instead of going to Hector he
got a pickaxe and spade, and proceeded to dig in the
trodden heap. At the first blow of the pickaxe he came upon
large stones, which were by no means easy to clear. After
working for a half hour, and only getting out two large and a
dozen smaller ones, Willie resolved to ask Sandy Spelman to
help him. So he left his pickaxe with one point fast between
two stones, and ran to the shop.

Sandy was at work, but his father was quite willing to let
him go. Willie told them he was digging for a treasure, and
they all laughed over it. But at the same time Willie thought,
*Who knows? People have found treasures buried in old
places like that. The Antiquary did not—but he is only in a
story, not in a "high story"* (for that was Willie's derivation of
the word *history*). *The place sounds likely enough. Anyhow,
where's the harm in trying?*

They were both so eager—for Sandy liked the idea of digging in the ruins much better than the work he was at—that they set off at full speed the moment they were out of the shop, and never slackened until they stood panting by the anchored pickaxe, upon which Spelman pounced. Being stronger than Willie and more used to hard work, he had soon dislodged both the stones which held it. They were so large that the boys had to roll them out of the little chamber instead of lifting them. After that they got on better, and had soon piled a good heap of stones against the wall outside.

After tea they set to work again, and worked till the twilight grew dark about them—by which time they had brought the heap down to what seemed the original level of the floor. Still there were stones below, but what with fatigue and darkness, they were now compelled to stop. Sandy went home, after promising to come as early as he could in the morning. He was to call Willie, who was to leave the end of a string hanging out the staircase window, whose other end should pass through the keyhole of his door and be tied to his wrist.

Willie seemed to have hardly been in bed an hour, when he woke with his arm at full length, and the pulling was going on as if it would pull him out of bed. He tugged again in reply, and jumped up.

It was a lovely summer morning. The sun was a few yards up in the sky, the grass glittered with dew, and the birds sang as if they were singing their first and would sing their last. The whole air was filled with a cool odor as of blessed thoughts, and just warm enough to let Willie know that the noontide would be hot. And there was Sandy waiting in the street to help him dig for the treasure! They went straight to the scene of their labor.

Having removed a few more stones, they began to hear a curious sound, which they agreed was more like that of running water than anything else they could think of. Now, except for a well in the street just before the cottage, there was no water they knew of much nearer than the river, and they wondered a good deal.

At length Sandy's pickaxe got hold of a stone which he could not move. He tried another, and succeeded, but soon began to suspect that there was some masonry there. Contenting himself therefore with clearing out only the loose stones, he soon found plainly enough that he was working in a narrow space, around which there was a circular wall of solid stone and lime. The sound of running water was now clear enough, and the earth in the hole was very damp. Sandy had now dug down three or four feet below the floor.

"It's an old well," he said.

"Does it smell bad?" asked Willie, peeping down disappointed.

"Not a bit," answered Sandy.

"Then it's not stagnant," said Willie.

"You might have told that by your ears without troubling your nose," said Sandy. "Didn't you hear it running?"

"How can it be running when it's buried away down there?" asked Willie.

"How can it make a noise if it isn't running?" retorted Sandy.

Willie attempted no reply.

It was now serious work to get the stones up, for only Sandy's head was above the level of the ground. It was all he could do to lift some of the larger stones out of the hole, and Willie saw that he must find a way to give him some help. He ran to the house and brought back a rope. One end of it Sandy tied around whatever stone was too heavy for him, and Willie, laying hold of the other, lifted along with him. They got on faster now, and in a few minutes Sandy exclaimed, "Here it is at last!"

"The treasure?" cried Willie. "Oh, jolly!"

Sandy burst out laughing, and shouted, "The water!"

"Bother the water!" growled Willie. "But go on, Sandy—the iron chest may be at the bottom of the water, you know."

"All very well for you up there!" retorted Sandy. "But though I can get the stones out, I can't get the water out. And I've no notion of diving where there's pretty sure to be nothing to dive for. Besides, a body can't dive in a stone pipe like this. I should want weights to sink me, and I mightn't get them off in time. I want my breakfast dreadful, Willie."

So saying, he scrambled up the side of the well, and his boots bore testimony to his having reached the water. Willie peered down into the well, and caught the dull glimmer of it through the stones. Then, a good deal disappointed, he followed Sandy as he strode away toward the house.

"You'll come and have your breakfast with me, Sandy, won't you?" he asked from behind him.

"No, thank you," answered Sandy. "I don't like any porridge but my mother's." And without looking behind him, he walked away home.

Before Willie had finished his porridge, he had gotten over his disappointment, and had even begun to see that he had never really expected to find a treasure. Only it would have been fun to hand it over to his father!

All through morning school, however, his thoughts would go back to the little vault, so cool and shadowy, sheltering its ancient well from the light that lorded it over all the country outside. No doubt the streams rejoiced in it, but even for them it would be too much before the evening came to cool and console them; while the slow wells in the marshy ground up on the mountains must feel faint in an hour of its burning eye. This well had always been, and always would be, cool and blessed and sweet. And wasn't it a nice thing to have a well of your own? Tibby needn't go any more to the village pump—which certainly was nearer, but stood in the street, not in their own ground. Of course, as yet, she could not draw a bucketful, for the water hardly came above the stones. Willie would soon get out as many as would make it deep enough—only, if it was all Sandy and he could do to get out the big ones, how was he to manage it alone?

He thought of something he and Hector had talked about some time before. After those two had gone as far in astronomy as they could understand, they found they were getting themselves into what seemed quite a jungle of planets, and suns, and comets, and constellations.

"It seems to me," said the shoemaker, "that to understand anything you must understand everything."

So they laid the book aside for the present. Hector, searching about for another book with which to fill up the remainder of the afternoons, came upon one in which the mechanical powers were treated after a simple fashion.

Of this book Willie had now read a good deal. He had not yet come to understand the mechanical power so thoroughly as to see that the lever and the wheel-and-axle are the same in kind, or that the screw, the inclined plane, and the wedge are the same power in different shapes. But he did understand that while a single pulley gives you no advantage except by enabling you to apply your strength in the most effective manner, a second pulley takes half the weight off you. Hence, with the difficulty in which he now found himself, came at once the thought of a block with a pulley in it, which he had seen lying about in the carpenter's shop. He remembered also that there was a great iron staple or eye in the vault just over the well, and if he could only get hold of a second pulley, the thing was as good as done—the well as good as cleared out to whatever depth he could reach below the water.

As soon as school was over, Willie ran to Mr. Spelman, and found to his delight that he could lend him not only the pulley but another as well. Each ran in a block which had an iron hook attached to it. With the aid of a ladder, Willie put the hook of one of the blocks through the staple, and then fastened the end of his rope to the block. Next he pulled off his shoes, got another bit of rope, and tied it around the largest stone within reach, loosely enough to allow the hook of the second pulley to lay hold of it. Then, as a sailor would say, he rove* the end of the long rope through this block, and getting up on the ladder again, rove it also through the first block hanging to the staple. Then Willie stood by the well and hauled away at the rope. It came slipping through the pulleys, and up rose the stone as if by magic. As soon as it came clear of the edge, he drew it toward him, lowered it to the ground, took off its rope collar, and rolled it out of the doorway. Then he got into the well again, tied the collar about another stone, drew down the pulley, thrust its hook through the collar, got out of the well, and hauled up the second stone.

In this way he had soon fetched out so many stones that he was standing far above his ankles in the water, which was so cold that he was glad to get out to pull up every stone. By this time it was perfectly explained how the water made a noise, for he saw it escape by an opening in the side of the well.

He came at last to a huge stone, round which with difficulty he managed to fasten the rope. He had to pull away smaller stones from beneath it, and pass the rope through under it. Having lifted it a little way with the powerful help of his tackle, to try if all was right before he got out to haul in earnest, he saw that his knot was slipping, and lowered the stone again so as to set it on one end, leaning against the side of the well. Then he discovered that his rope collar had frayed, and one of the strands was cut through; it would probably break and let the stone fall again into the well, and he would still more probably tumble after it. Willie was getting tired too, and it was growing very dusky in the ruins.

He thought it better to postpone further proceedings, and so climbed out of the well, caught up his shoes and stockings, and went into the house.

CHAPTER NINE
A Marvel

Early the next morning Dr. MacMichael, as he was dressing, heard a laugh of strange delight in the garden. He drew up the blind and looked out. There, some distance off, stood Willie, the one moment staring motionless at something at his feet, the other dancing and skipping and singing, but still looking down at something at his feet. His father could not see what this something was, for Willie was on the other side of one of the mounds. Dr. MacMichael was turning away to finish dressing, when from another direction a peculiar glitter caught his eye.

What can that mean? he said to himself. *Water in the garden! There's been no rain, and there's neither river nor reservoir to overflow!*

He hurried on the remainder of his clothes, and went out. But he had not gone many steps when what should he meet but a merry little brook coming cantering down between two of the mounds! It had already worn itself a channel in the path. He followed it up, wondering much, bewildered indeed. He had reached a little turfy hollow, down the middle of which it came bubbling and gabbling along, when Willie caught sight of him, and bounded to meet him with a radiant countenance and almost inarticulate cries of delight.

"Am I awake, Willie, or am I dreaming?" he asked.

"Wide awake, Papa," answered Willie.

"Then what *is* the meaning of this! *You* seem to be in on

the secret. Where does this water come from? I feel as if I were in a fairy tale."

"Isn't it lovely?" cried Willie. "I'll show you where it comes from. This way. You'll spoil your boots there. Look at the rhubarb bed—it's turned into a swamp."

"The garden will be ruined," said his father.

"No, no, Papa—we won't let it come to that. I've been watching it. There's no soil carried away yet. Do come and see."

In mute astonishment his father followed.

The ground was very uneven, with many heights and hollows, and the water took an amazing number of twists and turns. Willie led his father as straight as he could, but they crossed the little brook several times before they came to where, from the old stone shaft, like the crater of a volcano, it rolled over the brim, an eruption of cool, clear, lucid water. Plenteous it rose and overflowed, like a dark yet clear molten gem, tumbling itself into the open world. How deliciously wet it looked in the shadow! How it caught the sun the moment it left the chamber, grew merry, and trotted and trolled and cantered along!

"Is this *your* work, Willie?" asked his father, who did not know which of twenty questions to ask first.

"Mostly," said Willie.

"You little wizard! What have you been about? I can't understand it. We must make a drain for it at once."

"Bury a beauty like that in a drain!" cried Willie. "Oh, Papa!"

"Well, I don't know what else to do with it. How is it that it never found its way out before?"

"I'll soon show you that," said Willie. "I'll soon send it about its business."

Willie had thought, when he first saw the issuing water, that the weight of the fallen stones and the hard covering of earth being removed, the spring had burst out with tenfold volume and vigor. But he had now satisfied himself that the cause of the overflow must be the great stone he had set leaning against the side the last thing before dropping work the previous night: it must have blocked up the opening, and prevented the water from getting out as fast as before, that is, as fast as the spring rose. Therefore he now laid hold of the rope, which was still connected with the stone, and, not aware of how the water would help him by floating it, was astonished to find how easily he moved it. At once it swung away from the side into the middle of the well; the water ceased to run over the edge, with a loud gurgling began to sink, and sank down and down and down until the opening by which it escaped was visible.

"Ah! Now I understand!" cried Dr. MacMichael. "It's the old well of the Priory you've come upon, you little burrowing mole."

"Sandy helped me with the stones. I thought there might be a treasure down there, and that set me digging. It was a funny treasure to find, wasn't it? No treasure could have been prettier though."

"If this be the Prior's Well, and all be true they said about it in old times," returned his father, "it may turn out a greater treasure than you even hoped for, Willie. Why, as I found some time ago in an old book about the monasteries of the country, people used to come from great distances to drink the water of the Prior's Well, believing it a cure for every disease under the sun. Run into the house and fetch me a jug."

"Yes, Papa," said Willie, and bounded off.

There was no little brook careering through the garden now—only a few pools here and there, and its channel would soon be dry in the hot sun. But Willie thought how delightful it was to be able to have one there whenever he pleased. And it might be a much bigger brook too, for, instead of using the stone which could but partly block the water from the underground way, he would cut a piece of wood large enough to cover the opening, and rounded a little to fit the side of the well; then he would put the big stone just so far from the opening that the piece of wood could get through between it and the side of the well, and so be held tight. Then all the water would be forced to mount up, to get out at the top, and run through the garden.

Meantime Dr. MacMichael, having gone to see what course the water had taken, and how it had left the garden, found that, after a very circuitous route, it had run through the hedge into a surface drain in the field, and so down the hill toward the river.

When Willie brought him the jug, he filled it from the well, and carried the water into his surgery. There he put a little into several different glasses, dropped something out of one bottle into one glass and something out of another bottle into another glass, and soon satisfied himself that it contained medicinal salts in considerable quantities. There could be no doubt that Willie had found the Prior's Well.

"It's a good thing," said his father at breakfast, "that you didn't flood the house, Willie! One turn more and the stream would have been in at the back door."

"It wouldn't have done much harm," said Willie. "It would have run along the slabs in the passage and out again, for the front door is lower than the back. It would have been such fun!"

"You mischievous little thing!" said his mother, pretending to scold him. "You don't think what trouble you would have given Tibby!"

"But wouldn't it have been fun? And lovely, running through the house all the hot summer day?"

"There may be a difference of opinion about that, Willie," said his mother. "You, for instance, might like to walk through water every time you went from the parlor to the kitchen, but I can't say that I should."

Curious to know whether the village pump might not be supplied from the well, Dr. MacMichael next analyzed the water of that also, and satisfied himself that there was no connection between them. Within the next fortnight Willie discovered that as often as the stream ran through the garden, the little brook in which he had set his waterwheel went nearly dry.

He had soon made a nice little channel for the stream, so that it should not get into any of the beds. He laid down turf along its banks in some parts, and sowed grass and daisy seed in others. When he found a pretty stone or shell, or bit of colored glass or bright crockery or broken mirror, he would always throw it in, that the water might have the prettier path to run upon. Indeed, he emptied his store of marbles into it. He was not particularly fond of playing with marbles, but he had a great fancy for those of real white marble with lovely red streaks, and had collected some twenty or thirty of them. He kept them in the brook now, instead of in a calico bag.

The summer was a very hot and dry one. More than any of the rest of the gardens in the village, that of the Ruins suffered from such weather; not only was there a deep gravel bed under its mould, but a good part of its produce grew on the mounds, which were mostly heaps of stones, and neither gravel nor stones could retain much moisture. Willie watered it a good deal out of Prior's Well—but it was hard work, and did not seem to be of much use.

One evening he had set the little brook free to run through the garden. The sun was setting huge and red, with the promise of another glowing day tomorrow, and the air was stifling, and not a breath of wind stirring, so that the flowers hung their heads oppressed, and the leaves and little buttons of fruit on the trees looked ready to shrivel up and drop from the boughs. The thought came to Willie whether he could not turn the brook into a little Nile, causing it to overflow its banks and enrich the garden. He could not, of course, bring it about in the same way, for the Nile overflows from the quantities of rain up in the far-off mountains, making huge torrents rush into it faster than its channel, through a slow, level country that can carry the water away, so that there is nothing for it but overflow.

If, however, he could not make more water run out of the well, he could make it more difficult for what did come from it to get away. First, he stopped up the outlet through the hedge with stones and clay and bits of board; then watched as it spread, until he saw where it would try to escape next, and did the same; and so on, taking special care to keep it from the house. The mounds were a great assistance to him in hemming it in, but he had hard enough work of it notwithstanding. At one spot he saw that it would get the better of him in a few minutes, and make straight for the back door.

He ran at once and opened the sluice* in the well, and away the stream gurgled underground.

Before morning the water it left had all disappeared. It had soaked through the mounds, and into the gravel, but comforting the hot roots as it went, and feeding them with dissolved minerals. Doubtless, also, it lay all night in many a little hidden pool, which the heat of the next day's sun drew up, comforting again, through the roots in the earth, and through the leaves in the air, up into the sky.

Willie could not help thinking that the garden looked refreshed. The green was brighter, he thought, and the flowers held up their heads a little better. The carrots looked more feathery, and the ferns more palmy—everything looked, he said, just as he felt after a good drink out of the Prior's Well. At all events, he resolved to do the same every night after sunset while the hot weather lasted, unless his father had an objection.

Dr. MacMichael said he might try it, only he must not go to bed and leave the water running, or else they would have a cartload of mud in the house before morning.

So Willie strengthened and heightened his barriers, and built a huge one at the last point where the water had tried to get away. As soon as the sun went down, he shut the sluice, and watched the water as it surged up in the throat of the well, and rushed out to be caught in the toils he had made for it. Before it could find a fresh place to get out at, the whole upper part of the garden was one network of lakes and islands.

Willie kept walking round and round it, as if it had been a wild beast trying to get out of its cage, and he had to watch and prevent it at every weak spot—or as if he were a magician, busily sustaining the charm by which he confined the gadabout creature. The moment he saw it beginning to get the better of him, he ran to the sluice and banished it to the regions below. Then he fetched an old newspaper, sat down on the borders of his lake, fashioned boat after boat out of the paper, and sent them sailing like merchant ships from isle to blooming isle.

Night after night Willie flooded the garden, and always before morning the water had sunk away through the gravel. There was no doubt that everything was mightily refreshed by it. The look of exhaustion and hopelessness was gone, and life was busy in flower and tree and plant. This year there was not a garden, even on the banks of the river, to compare with it. When the autumn came, the garden produced more fruit than Dr. MacMichael remembered ever seeing before.

CHAPTER TEN

A New Alarm

Willie was always thinking what uses he could put things to. Only he was never tempted to set a fine thing to do dirty work, as dull-hearted money-grubbers do—mill-owners, for instance, when they make the channel of a lovely mountain stream serve for a drain to carry off the filth from their works. Willie made the prisoned stream work for the garden, and now he made the running stream work for himself.

Ever since he had ceased being night nurse to little Agnes, he had wished that he had someone to wake him in the middle of every night, that he might get up and look out of the window. For, after he had fed his baby sister and given her back to his mother in a state of contentment, before getting into bed again he had always looked out of the window to see what the night was like. He was not anxious about the weather, for he could enjoy weather of any sort and all sorts, but he merely wanted to see what Madame Night was thinking about—how she looked, and what she was doing. He found her such a changeful creature that every time he looked at her, she looked at him with a different face.

Before he had made this acquaintance with the night, he would often, before he fell asleep, lie wondering what he was going to dream about. Willie was very fond of dreaming, but after he had begun to make acquaintance with her, he would just as often fall asleep wondering what the day would be dreaming about—for, in his own fanciful way of thinking, he had settled that the look of the night was what the day was dreaming. Hence, when Agnes required his services no longer, he fell asleep the first night with the full intention of waking just as before, and getting up to have a peep into the day's dream, whatever it might be, that night, and every night thereafter. But he was now back in his own room, and there was nothing to wake him, so he slept soundly until the day had done dreaming and the morning was wide awake. Neither had he awoken any night since, or seen what marvel there might be beyond his window panes.

What can be going on when we are asleep? Sometimes the stars are busy, and sometimes the moon, sometimes the clouds, sometimes the wind, sometimes the snow, sometimes the frost—and sometimes all of them together. Sometimes the owl and the moth and the beetle, and the bat and the cat and the rat are all at work. Sometimes there are flowers in bloom that love the night better than the day, and are busy through the darkness pouring out on the still air the scent they withheld during the sunlight. Sometimes the lightning and thunder, sometimes the moon rainbow, sometimes the aurora borealis* are busy. And the streams are running all night long, and seem to babble louder than in the daytime, for the noises of the working world are still, so that we hear the night noises better. But it was the *look* of the night, the meaning on her face that Willie cared most about, and desired so much to see, although ever so many strange and lovely dreams might be passing before his window. He often dreamed that he had waked up, and was looking out on some gorgeous and lovely show, but in the morning he knew sorrowfully that he had only dreamed his own dream, not gazed into that of the sleeping day.

Again and again he had worked his brains to weariness, trying to invent some machine that should wake him. But although he was older and more clever now, he fared no better than when he had wanted to wake himself to help his mother with Agnes. He must have some motive power before he could do anything, and the clock was still the only power he could think of. Yet he was afraid to meddle with the clock, for its works were beyond him, and it was so essential to the well-being of the house that he would not venture putting it in jeopardy.

One day, however, when Willie was thinking nothing about it, it struck him that he had another motive power at his command. His motive power was the stream from the Prior's Well, and the means of using it for his purpose stood on a shelf in the Ruins, in the shape of the toy waterwheel which he had laid aside as distressingly useless.

First of all, Willie made a second bit of channel for the stream, like a little loop to the first, so that he could, when he pleased, turn a part of the water into it, and let it join the principal channel a little lower down. This was his millrace. Just before it joined the older part again, right opposite his window, he made it run for a little way in a direct line toward the house, and in this part of the new channel he made preparation for his waterwheel. Into the channel he laid a piece of iron pipe, which had been lying about useless for years. Just where the water would issue in a concentrated rush from the lower end of it, he constructed a foundation for his wheel. The water, as it issued from the pipe, should strike straight upon its floats, and send it whirling around. It took Willie some time to build it, for he wanted this to be a good and permanent job. He had stones at his command, and he had a well, he said, that yielded both stones and water, which was more than everybody could say. In order to make it a sound bit of work, he fetched a lump of quick-lime* from the kiln, where they burned quantities of it to scatter over the clay soil. He wet it with water till it fell into powder, and then mixed it with sand which he riddled from the gravel he dug from the garden, and made it into good strong mortar.

When its bed was at length made for it, he took the wheel and put in a longer axle, to project on one side beyond the gudgeon block, and upon this projecting piece he fixed a large reel. Then, having put the wheel in its place, he asked his father for sixpence,* part of which he spent for a large ball of pack thread. The outside end of the ball he fastened to the reel, then threw the ball through the open window into his room, and there undid it from the inside end, laying the thread in coils on the floor. When it was time to go to bed, he ran out and turned the water first into the garden, and then into the new channel. The wheel suddenly began to spin about and wind the pack thread onto the reel. He ran to his room, undressed quickly, tied the other end of the thread about his wrist, and fell fast asleep. He dreamed that the thread had waked him, and drawn him to the window, where he saw the waterwheel flashing like a fire wheel, and the water rushing away from it in a green flame.

But when he did awake it was broad day, and the coils of pack thread were still lying on the floor. The brook was singing in the garden, and when he went to the window, he saw the wheel spinning merrily round. He dressed in haste, ran out, and found that the thread had tangled among the bushes on its way to the wheel, and had stuck fast. The wheel had broken it to get loose, and had been spinning uselessly round and round all night for nothing.

That afternoon he set poles up for guides, along the top of which the thread might run, and so keep clear of the bushes. But he fared no better the next night, for he never waked till morning. He found that the wheel stood stock still, for the thread had filled the reel, slipped off, wound itself about the wheel, and choked it in many windings. Indeed, the thread was in a wonderful tangle about the whole machine, and it took him a long time to unwind—turning the wheel backward, so as not to break the thread.

In order to remove the cause of this fresh failure, he went

to the turner,* whose name was William Burt, and asked him to turn for him a large reel or spool, with deep ends and a small cylinder between. William told him he was very busy just then, but he would fix a suitable piece of wood for him on his old lathe,* with which he might turn what he wanted for himself. This was Willie's first attempt at the use of the turning-lathe, but he had often watched Burt at work, and the result was tolerably satisfactory. Burt finished it off for him with just a few touches. Willie, delighted with his acquisition of the rudiments of a new trade, carried the spool home with him, to try once more to make his waterwheel into a watchman.

That night the pull did indeed come, but, alas, before Willie had even fallen asleep. The spool had gone flying round, and had swallowed up the thread incredibly fast. He made haste to get the end off his wrist, and saw it fly through the little hole in the window frame, and away after the rest of it, to be wound on the whirling wheel.

Something seemed to be always going wrong! He concluded that it was a difficult thing to make a machine which should do just what the maker wished.

Disappointing as this was, however, there was progress in it. Willie had gotten the thing to work, and all that remained was to regulate it. But this turned out to be the most difficult part of all. He saw at once that if he were to only make the thread longer, he would increase the constant danger there was of getting fouled, not to mention the awkwardness of using such a quantity of it. If the kitten were to get into the room, for instance, after he had laid it down, she would ruin his every hope for the time being. More string would cost money, and in Willie's eyes sixpence was a huge sum to ask from his father. But if he could make the machine wind more slowly, he might then be able to shorten instead of lengthen the string.

After much pondering, he saw that if, instead of the spool,

he were to fix on the axle a small cogged wheel—that is, a wheel with teeth—and then make these cogs fit into the cogs of a much larger wheel, the small wheel, which would turn once with every turn of the waterwheel, must turn a great many times before it could turn the big wheel once. Then he must fix the spool on the axis of this great slow wheel, when, turning only as often as the big wheel turned, the spool would wind the thread much more slowly.

At last Willie was entirely successful in timing his machine, for the run of water was always the same, and he could tell exactly how much thread it would wind in a given time. Having then measured off the thread with a mark of ink for the first hour, two for the second, and so on, he was able to set his alarm according to the time at which he wished to be wakened by the pull at his wrist.

But if anyone happened to go into the garden after the household was asleep, and had come upon the toy waterwheel working away in the starlight or moonlight, how little, even if he had caught sight of the nearly invisible thread, and had discovered that the wheel was winding it up, would he have seen what the machine was about? How little would he have thought that its business was with the infinite; that it was in connection with the window of an eternal world— namely, Willie's soul—from which at a given moment it would lift the curtains of his eyelids, and let the night of the outer world in upon the thought and feeling of the boy.

One night as he came home from visiting a patient, Dr. MacMichael did come upon the wheel, and was just going to turn the water off at the well, when he caught sight of the winding thread.

What can this be now? he said to himself. *Some new freak of Willie's, of course. Yes, the thread goes right up to his window! I dare say if I were to stop and watch I should see something happen.*

Just then the wheel stopped. The next moment the blind

of Willie's window was drawn up, and there stood Willie, his face and his white gown glimmering in the moonlight. He caught sight of his father, and up went the sash.

"O Papa!" he cried. "I didn't think it was you I was going to see!"

"Who was it then you thought to see?" asked his father.

"Oh, nobody—only the night herself, and the moon perhaps."

"What new freak of yours is this, my boy?" asked his father, smiling.

"Wait a minute, and I'll tell you all about it," answered Willie. Out he came in his nightshirt, his bare feet dancing with pleasure at having his father for his midnight companion. On the grass, beside the ruins, in the moonlight, by the gurgling water, Willie told him all about it.

"Yes, my boy, you are right," said his father. "God never sleeps—and it would be a pity if we never saw Him at His night work."

CHAPTER ELEVEN
What Willie Saw

The little mill went on night after night waking Willie—almost every night in the summer, and those nights in the winter when the frost had not frozen the machinery.

Sometimes, when he looked out, it was a simple, quiet, thoughtful night that met his gaze, without any moon, but as full of stars as it could hold, all flashing and trembling through the dew that was slowly sinking down the air to settle upon the earth and its thousand living things below. On such a night Willie never went to bed again without wishing to be pure in heart, that he might one day see God whose thought had taken the shape of such a lovely night. For although he could not have expressed himself thus at that time, he felt that it must be God's thinking that put it all there.

Other times, the stars would be half blotted out—all over the heavens—not with mist, but with the light of the moon. Oh, how lovely she was! So calm! So alone in the midst of the great blue ocean—the sun of the night! She seemed to hold up the tent of the heavens in a great silver knot. And, like the stars above, all the flowers below had lost their color and looked pale and wan, sweet and sad.

Several times in winter Willie saw the air so full of great snowflakes that he could not see the moon through them, although her light was visible all about them. They came floating slowly down through the dusky light, just as if they had precipitated from that solution of moonbeams. He could hardly persuade himself to go to bed, but the cold soon drove him to his nest again.

Once the wheel watchman pulled him up in the midst of a terrible thunderstorm. The East and the West were answering each other with alternate flashes of forked lightning that seemed to split the black clouds with cracks of blinding blue, awful in their blasting silence—followed by great, billowy, shattering rolls of thunder, as loud as if the sky had been a huge kettle drum on which the clubs of giant drummers were beating a terrible onset. And at sudden intervals the big-dropped rain pattered to the earth as if beaten out of the clouds by the blows of the thunder. But Willie was not frightened, though the lightning blinded and thunder deafened him—not frightened any more than the tiniest flower in the garden below, which, if she could have thought about it, would have thought it all being done only that she might feel cooler and stronger and be able to hold up her head better.

And once Willie saw the glorious dance of the aurora borealis in all the colors of a faint rainbow. The frosty snow sparkled underneath, and the cold stars of winter sparkled above, and between the snow and the stars shimmered and shifted, vanished and came again, a serried host of spears. Willie had been reading *Paradise Lost,* and the part which pleased him most was the wars of the angels. Hence the aurora looked to him like the crowding of innumerable spears—in the hands of angels, themselves invisible—clashed together and shaken asunder, however, as in the convolutions of a mazy dance of victory, rather than brandished and hurtled as in the tumult of the battle.

Another delightful vision was far more common: the moon wading through clouds blown slowly across the sky, especially if by an upper wind, unfelt below. Now she would be sinking helplessly in a black faint—growing more and more dim, until at last she disappeared from the night, and was blotted from the face of nature, leaving only a dim memorial light behind her. Then her soul would come into her again, and with a slow solemn revival, her light would grow and grow until the last fringe of the great cloud swung away from off her face, and she dawned out stately and glorious to float for a space in queenly triumph across a lake of clearest blue. And Willie was philosopher enough to say to himself that all this fainting and reviving, all this defeat and conquest, were but appearances—that the moon was her own bright self all the time, basking contented in the light of her sun, between it and her the cloud could not creep, only between her and Willie.

But what delighted him most of all was to catch the moon dreaming. That was when the old moon, tumbled over on her back, would come floating up the east, like a little boat on the rising tide of the night, looking lost on the infinite sea. Dreaming she must be, for she seemed to care about nothing—not even that she was old and worn, and withered and dying—not even that, instead of sinking down in the west, into some deep bed of dim repose, she was drifting, haggard and battered, untidy and weak and sleepy, up and up into the dazzling halls of the sun. Did she know that his light would clothe her as with a garment, and hide her in the highest recesses of his light-filled ceiling? Or was it only that she was dreaming sweet, cool, tender dreams of her own, and neither knew nor cared about anything around her? What a strange look all the night wore while the tired old moon was thus dreaming of the time when she would come again, back through the vanishing and the darkness— a single curved thread of a baby moon.

There were many other nights, far more commonplace, which Willie liked yet could not keep him long from his bed. There was the moonless and cloudy night, when, if he had been able to pierce the darkness to the core, he would have found nothing but blackness. It had a power of its own, but not much to look at. On such a night he would say to himself that the day was so sound asleep she was dreaming of nothing at all, and so make haste to his nest again. Then there were the cold nights of black frost, when there was cloud enough to hide the stars and the moon, and yet a little light came soaking through, enough to reveal how hopeless and dreary the earth was. For in such nights of cold, when there is no snow to cover them, the flowers that have crept into their roots to hide from the winter are not even able to dream of the spring, but may only sleep. He never could look long at such a night.

Neither did he care to look long when a loud wind was out—except the moon was bright, for the most he could distinguish was the trees blowing against the sky, and they always seemed not to like it, and to want to stop. And if the big strong trees did not like it, how could the poor little delicate flowers, shivering and shaking and tossed to and fro? If he could have seen the wind itself, it would have been a different thing, but as it was, he could enjoy it more by lying in bed and listening to it. Then as he listened he could fancy himself floating out through miles and miles of night and wind, and moon-and-starlight, or moony snowflakes, or even thick darkness and rain; until, falling asleep in the middle of his fancy, it would thicken around him into a dream of delight.

Once there was to be an eclipse of the moon about two o'clock in the morning.

"It's a pity it's so late, or rather so early, Willie," said Dr. MacMichael. "You won't be able to see it."

"Oh, yes, I shall, Father," answered Willie.

"I can't let you sit up so late. I shall be in the middle of Sedgy Moor most likely when it begins—and who is to wake you? I won't have your mother disturbed, and Tibby's not much to depend upon. She's too hard-worked to wake when she likes, poor old thing."

"Oh, I can be awakened without anybody to do it!" said Willie.

"You don't mean you can depend on your waterwheel to wake you at the right time, do you?"

"Yes, I do, Father."

"Well, it *will* be worth something to you, if it can do that!" said Dr. MacMichael.

"It's been worth a great deal to me, already," said Willie. "It would have shown me an eclipse before now, only there hasn't been one since I set it going."

And wake him it did. While his father was riding across the moor, in the strange hush of the blotted moon, Willie was out in the garden beside his motionless wheel, watching the fell shadow of the earth passing over the blessed face of the moon, and leaving her pure and clear and nothing worse.

CHAPTER TWELVE

A New Scheme

"I've had a letter from my mother, John," said Mrs. MacMichael to her husband one day at dinner. "It's wonderful how well she manages to write, when she sees so poorly."

"She might see well enough—at least a great deal better— if she would submit to an operation," said the doctor.

"At *her* age, John!" returned his wife in an expostulatory tone. "Do you really think it worthwhile for the few years that are left her?"

"Worthwhile to see well for a few years!" exclaimed the doctor. "Indeed, I do."

"But there's another thing I want to talk to you about now," said Mrs. MacMichael. "Since old Ann's death six months ago, she says she has been miserable, and if she goes on like this, it will shorten the few days that are left her. Effie, the only endurable servant she has had since Ann, is going to leave at the end of her half-year, and she says the thought of another makes her wretched. My mother may be a little hard to please, but after being used to one for so many years, it is no wonder if she is particular. I don't know what is to be done."

"I don't know, either—except you make her a present of Tibby," said her husband.

"John!" exclaimed Mrs. MacMichael, and he burst out laughing.

"You don't think they'd pull together?" he said.

"Two old people—each with her own ways, and without any memories in common to bind them together! I'm surprised at your dreaming of such a thing!"

"But I didn't even dream of it; I only said it," returned her husband. "It's time you knew when I was joking, Wifie."

"You joke so dreadfully like earnest!" she answered.

"If only we had one more room in the house!" said the doctor, thoughtfully.

"Ah!" returned his wife eagerly. "That would be a blessing! And though Tibby would be a thorn in every inch of Mamma's body if they were alone together, I have no doubt they would get on very well with me between them."

"I don't doubt it," said her husband, still thoughtfully.

"Couldn't we manage it somehow, John?" said Mrs. MacMichael, half timidly, after a pause of some duration.

"I can't say I see how—at this moment," answered the doctor, "much as I should like it. But there's time yet, and we'll think it over, and talk about it, and perhaps we may hit upon some plan or other. Most things *may* be done, and everything necessary *can* be done *somehow*. So we won't bother our minds about it, but only for our brains, and see what they can do for us."

With this he rose and went to his laboratory.

Willie rose also, and went straight to his own room. Having looked all around it thoughtfully several times, he went out again on the landing, where a ladder led up into a garret running the whole length of the roof of the cottage.

"My room would do for Grannie," he said to himself, "and I could sleep up there. A shakedown* in the corner would do well enough for me."

He climbed the ladder, pushed open the trapdoor, crept half through, and surveyed the gloomy place.

"There's no window but a skylight!" he said, and his eyes smarted as if the tears were about to rush into them. "What *shall* I do? Wheelie will be useless! Well, I can't help it—and if I can't help it, I can bear it. To have Grannie comfortable will be better than to look out of the window ever so much."

He drew in his head, came down the ladder with a rush, and hurried off to school.

At supper he laid his scheme before his father and mother. They looked very much pleased with their boy, but his father said at once, "No, no, Willie, it won't do. I'm glad you've been the first to think of something—only, unfortunately, your plan won't work. You can't sleep there."

"I'll engage to sleep wherever there's room to lie down—and if there isn't, I'll engage to sleep sitting or standing," said Willie, whose mother had often said she wished she could sleep like Willie. "And as I don't walk in my sleep," he added, "the trapdoor needn't be shut."

"Mice, Willie!" said his mother, in a tone of much significance.

"The cat and I are good friends," returned Willie. "She'll be pleased enough to sleep with me."

Then his father said, "Even if I were at the expense of ceiling the whole roof with lath and plaster, we should find you some morning in summer baked black as a coal—or else, some morning in winter frozen so stiff that, when we tried to lift you, your arm snapped off like a dry twig."

"Ho! Ho! Ho!" laughed Willie. "Then there would be the more room for Grannie."

His father laughed with him, but his mother looked a little shocked.

"No, Willie," said his father again. "You must make another attempt."

Willie lay so long awake that night, thinking, that his wheel pulled him up before he had had a wink of sleep. He got up, of course, and looked from the window.

The day was dreaming grandly. The sky was pretty clear in front, and full of sparkles of light, for the stars were kept in the background by the moon, which was down a little toward the west. She had sunk below the top of a huge towering cloud, the edges of whose jags and pinnacles she bordered with a line of silvery light. Now this cloud rose into the sky from just behind the ruins, and looking a good deal like upheaved towers and spires, made Willie think within himself what a grand place the priory must have been, when its roofs and turrets rose up into the sky.

"They say a lot of people lived in it then!" he thought with himself as he stood gazing at the cloud.

Suddenly he gave a great jump, and clapped his hands so loud that he woke his father.

"Is anything the matter, my boy?" he asked, opening Willie's door and peeping in.

"No, Papa, nothing," answered Willie. "Only something that came into my head with a great bounce!"

"Ah! Where did it come from, Willie?"

"Out of that cloud there. Isn't it a grand one?"

"Certainly grand enough to put many thoughts into a body's head, Willie. What did it put into yours?"

"Please, I would rather not tell just yet," answered Willie, "if you don't mind, Father."

"Not a bit, my boy. Tell me just when you please, or don't tell me at all. I should like to hear it, but only at your pleasure, Willie."

"Thank you, Father. I do want to tell you, you know, but not just yet."

"Very well, my boy. Now go to bed, and sleep may better the thought before morning."

Willie soon fell asleep, for he now believed he had found what he wanted. He was up earlier than usual the next morning, and out in the garden.

Surely, he said to himself, *those ruins, which once held so many monks, might manage even yet to find a room for me!*

He went wandering about them, like an undecided young bird looking for the very best possible spot to build its nest in. The spot Willie sought was that which would require the least labor and material to make into a room.

Before Tibby called him to his porridge, he had fixed upon one. All the time between morning and afternoon school, he spent in the same place—and when he came home in the evening, he was accompanied by Mr. Spelman, who went with him straight to the ruins. They were there a good while together, and when Willie at length came in, his mother saw that his face was more than usually radiant, and she was certain he had some new scheme or other in his head.

CHAPTER THIRTEEN
Willie's Nest

The spot Willie had fixed upon was in the part of the ruins next to the cottage, not many yards from its back door. There were still a few vaulted pieces on the ground level used by the family. The vault over the wood house was perfectly sound and weather tight, and therefore, as Willie and the carpenter agreed, quite safe to roost upon. In a corner outside, and now open to the elements, had once been a small winding stone stair, which led to the room above. It was just possible to climb on the few broken fragments projecting from the two sides of the corner, and so reach the top of the vault. Willie had often climbed up to look out through a small, flat-arched window into the garden of the manse. When Mr. Shepherd, the clergyman, who often walked in his garden, caught sight of him, he always came nearer and had a chat with him. He did not mind such people as Willie looking into his garden, and seeing what he was about. Sometimes also little Mona Shepherd, a girl of his own age, would be running about—and she also, if she caught sight of Willie, was sure to come hopping and skipping like a bird to have a talk with him, and beg him to take her up, which, as he assured her, was all but impossible.

To this place Mr. Spelman and Willie climbed, and there held consultation whether and how it could be made habitable. The main difficulty was, how to cover it—for although the walls were quite sound a long way up, it lay open to the sky. But about ten feet over their heads they saw the holes in two of the opposing walls where the joists* formerly sustaining the floor of the chamber above had rested. Mr. Spelman thought that, without any very large outlay either of time or material, he could lay a floor there, as it were, and then turn it into a roof by covering it with cement, or pitch, or something of the sort. For that he would take counsel with his friend Mortimer, the mason.

"But," said Willie, "that would turn it into the bottom of a cistern, for the walls above would hold the rain in, and what would happen then? Either it must gather till it reached the top, or the weight of it would burst the walls, or perhaps break through my roof and drown me."

"It is easy to avoid that," said Mr. Spelman. "We have only to lay on the cement a little thicker at one side, and slope the surface down to the other, where a hole through the wall, with a pipe in it, would let the water off."

"I know!" cried Willie. "That's what they called a gargoyle!"

"I don't know anything about that," said the carpenter. "I know it will carry off the water."

"To be sure," said Willie. "It's capital."

"But," said Mr. Spelman, "it's rather too serious a job to set about before asking the doctor's leave. It will cost money."

"Much?" asked Willie, whose heart sank within him.

"Well, that depends on what you count much," answered Spelman. "All I can say is, it wouldn't be anything out of your father's pocket."

"I don't see how that can be," said Willie. "To cost money, and yet be nothing out of my father's pocket! *I've* only got threepence ha'penny."

"Your father and I will talk about it," said the carpenter mysteriously, and offered no further information.

There always seems to be some way of doing a thing, thought Willie. He little knew by what a roundabout succession of cause and effect his father's kindness to Spelman was at this moment returning to him, one of the links of connection being this project of Willie's own.

The carpenter called on the doctor later in the evening, and they had a long talk together. Spelman set forth his scheme, and the doctor listened in silence until he had finished.

"But," said Dr. MacMichael, "that will cost a good deal, I fear, and I have no money to spare."

"Dr. MacMichael," said Spelman solemnly, his long face looking as if some awful doom were about to issue from the middle of it, "you forget how much I am in your debt."

"No, I don't," returned the doctor. "But neither do I forget that it takes all your time and labor to provide for your family—and what will become of them if you set about this job, with no return in prospect but the satisfaction of clearing off an old debt?"

"It is very good of you, sir, to think of that," said the carpenter. "But, begging your pardon, I've thought of it too. Many's the time you've come after what I'd ha' called work hours to see my wife—yes, in the middle of the night, more than once or twice—and why shouldn't I do the same? Look ye here, sir. If you're not in a main hurry, an' 'll give me time, I'll do the heavy work o' this job after six o'clock o' the summer nights, with Sandy to help me, and I'll charge you no more than a journeyman's wages by the hour. And what Willie and Sandy can do by themselves I'll not charge you for. And if you'll have the goodness, when I give you the honest time, at fourpence ha'penny an hour, just to strike that off my bill, I'll be more obliged to you than I am now. Only I fear I must make you pay for that material—not a farthing more than it costs me at the sawmills, up at the Grange, for the carriage'll come in with other lots I must have."

"It's a generous offer, Spelman," said the doctor, "and I

accept it heartily, though you are turning the tables of obligation upon me. You'll have done far more for me than I ever did for you."

"I wish that were true, sir, but it isn't. My wife's not a giantess yet, for all you've done for her."

Spelman set to work at once. New joists were inserted in the old walls, boarded over, and covered to keep out the water. Then a pipe was put through the wall to carry the water off—and if the pipe was not masked with an awful head, as the remains of more than one on the Priory showed it would have been in the days of the monks, yet it worked as faithfully without it.

When it came to plastering the walls, Mr. Spelman, after giving them full directions, left the two boys to do that between them. Although there was no occasion to roughen these walls by clearing away the old mortar from between the stones (for the weather had done that quite sufficiently), and all the preparation wanted for the first thin coat was a good washing, it took them a good many days, working all their time, to lay on the orthodox three coats of plaster. Mr. Spelman had wisely boarded the ceiling, so that they had not to plaster that.

Meantime he was preparing a door and window frames in the shop. The room had probably been one of the prior's, for it was much too large and lofty for a mere cell, and had two windows. But these were fortunately small, not like the splendid ones in the chapel and refectory,* else they would have been hard to fill with glass.

"I'm afraid you'll be starved with cold, Willie," said his father one day, after watching the boys at work for a few minutes. "There's no fireplace."

"Oh! That doesn't signify," answered Willie. "Look how thick the walls are! And I shall have plenty of blankets on my bed. Besides, we can easily put a little stove in, if it's wanted."

But when the windows were fitted and fixed, Dr. MacMichael saw to his dismay that they were not made to open. They had not even a pane upon hinges.

"This'll never do, Willie," he said. "This is far worse than no chimney."

Willie took his father by the coat, and led him to a corner where a hole went right through the wall into another room—if that can be called a room which had neither floor nor ceiling.

"There, Father!" he said. "I am going to fit a slide over this hole, and then I can let in just as much or as little air as I please."

"It would have been better to have at least one of the windows to open. You will only get the air from the ruins that way, whereas you might have had all the scents from Mr. Shepherd's flowers and roses."

"As soon as Mr. Spelman has done the job," said Wlllie, "I will make them both to open wide on hinges—but I don't want to bother him about it, for he has been very kind, and I can do it quite well myself."

This satisfied the father. At length the floor was boarded; a strong thick door was fitted tight; a winding stair of deal inserted where the stone one had been used, and cased in with planks, well pitched on the outside; and now Willie's mother was busy making little muslin curtains for his windows and a carpet for the middle of the floor.

In the meantime, his father and mother had both written to his grandmother, telling her how Willie had been using his powers both of invention and of labor to make room for her, and urging her to come and live with them, for they were all anxious to have her to take care of. But, in fact, small persuasion was necessary, for the old lady was only too glad to accept the invitation—and before the warm weather of autumn was over, she was ready to go to them.

By this time Willie's room was furnished. All the things

from his former nest had been moved into it: the bed with the chintz curtains, covered with strange flowers and birds; the old bureau, with the many drawers inside the folding cover, in which he kept all his little treasures; the table at which he read books that were too big to hold; the oblong mirror that hung on the wall, with an outspread gilt eagle at the top of it; the big old armchair that had belonged to his great-grandfather, who wrote his sermons in it. All the things the boy had about him were old, and in all his later life he never could bear new furniture. His grandmother's furniture began to appear, and a great cartload of it from her best bedroom was speedily arranged in Willie's late quarters. As soon as they were ready for her, Mrs. MacMichael set out in a hired carriage to fetch her mother.

CHAPTER FOURTEEN
Willie's Grandmother

Willie was in a state of excitement until his grandmother arrived, looking for her as eagerly as if she had been a princess. So few were the opportunities of traveling between Priory Leas and the town where his grandmother lived, that he had never seen her, and curiosity had its influence as well as affection. Great, therefore, was his delight when at last the chaise came around the corner of the street, and stopped at their door. The first thing he caught sight of was a curious bonnet, like a black coal-scuttle upside down. And inside that, when it turned its front toward him, he saw a close-fitting widow's cap, and inside that a kind old face, and if he could have looked still further, he would have seen a kind young soul inside the kind old face. She smiled sweetly when she saw him, but was too tired to take any further notice of him until she had had tea.

During that meal, Willie devoted himself to a silent waiting upon her, watching and trying to anticipate her every want. When she had eaten a little bread and butter and an egg, and drunk two cups of tea, she lay back in her own easy chair, which had been placed for her by the side of the parlor fire, and fell asleep for ten minutes, breathing so gently that Willie got frightened, and thought she was dead. But all at once she opened her eyes wide, amd made a sign to him to come to her.

"Sit down there," she said, pushing a little footstool toward him.

Willie obeyed, and sat looking up in her face.

"So," she said, "you're the little man that can do everything?"

"No, Grannie," answered Willie, laughing. "I wish I could, but I am only learning to do a few things, and there's not one of them I can do right yet."

"Anyhow, supposing you only half as clever a fellow as you pass for, I want to try you. Have you any objection to service? I should like to hire you for my servant—my own special servant, you understand."

"All right, Grannie. Here I am!" cried Willie, jumping up. "What shall I do first?"

"Sit down again instantly, and wait till we've finished the bargain. I must first have you understand that though I don't want to be hard on you, you must come when I call you, and do what I tell you."

"Of course, Grannie. Only I can't when I'm at school, you know."

"I don't have to be told that, and I'm not going to be a tyrant. But for all your cleverness, you've never asked me what wages I would give you."

"Oh! I don't want any wages, Grannie. I *like* to do things for people—and you're my very own grandmother."

"Well, I suppose I must settle your wages for you. I mean to pay you by the job. It's an odd arrangement for a servant, but it will suit me best. And as you don't ask any, I needn't pay you more than I like myself."

"Certainly not, Grannie. I'm quite satisfied."

"Meantime, no engagement of a servant ought to be counted complete without earnest."*

"I'm quite in earnest, Grannie," said Willie, who did not know this meaning of the word.

They all laughed.

"I don't see what's so funny," said Willie, laughing too, however.

But when they explained to him what *earnest* meant, then he laughed with understanding, as well as with good will.

"So," his grandmother went on, "I will give you earnest, which, you know, binds you my servant. But for how long, Willie?"

"Till you're tired of me, Grannie. Only, you know, I'm Papa and Mamma's servant first, and you may have to arrange with them sometimes—for what should I do if you were all to want me at once?"

"We'll easily manage that. I'll arrange with them, as you say. And now, here's your earnest."

As she spoke, she put into his hand what Willie took to be a shilling. But when he glanced at it, he found himself to be mistaken.

"Thank you, Grannie," he said, trying not to show himself a little disappointed, for he had had another scheme in his head for some days, and the shilling would have been everything toward that.

"Do you know what Grannie has given you, Willie?" said his mother.

"Yes, Mother—such a pretty brass medal!"

"Show it to me, dear. Why, Willie! It's no brass medal, child—it's a sovereign!"*

"No-o-o-o! Is it? O Grannie!" he cried, and went dancing about the room, as if he would actually fly with delight. Willie had never seen a sovereign, for that part of the country never saw gold money. To get it for him, his grandmother had had to send to the bank in the county town.

After this she would often give him a sixpence or a shilling, and sometimes even a half crown when she asked him to do anything she thought a little harder than usual. And so Willie now had plenty of money with which to carry out his little plans. When remonstrated by her daughter for giving him so much, his grandmother would say, "Look how the boy spends it! He's always doing something with it.

He never wastes it on sweets. Not he! My Willie's above that!"

The old lady generally spoke of him as if she were the chief if not the sole proprietor of the boy. "I'm sure I couldn't do better with it," she would add, "and that you'll see when he comes to be a man. He'll be the making of you all."

"But, Mother, you can't afford it."

"How do you know that? I can afford it very well. I've no house rent to pay, and I am certain it is the very best return I can make you for your kindness. What I do for Willie will prove to have been done for us all."

Certainly Willie's grandmother showed herself a very wise old lady. The wisest old ladies are always those with young souls looking out of their eyes. And few things pleased Willie more than waiting upon her. He had a passion for being useful, and as his grandmother needed his help more than anyone else, her presence in the house was an endless source of pleasure to him.

But his father grew anxious. He did not like her giving Willie so much money—not that he minded Willie having or spending the money, for he believed that the *spending* would keep the *having* from hurting him. But he feared lest through her gifts the purity of the boy's love for his grandmother might be injured, and the service which at first had looked only to her as its end might degenerate into a mere serving of her for the sake of her shillings.

Therefore, Dr. MacMichael had a long talk with her about it. She was indignant at the notion of the least danger of spoiling Willie, but so anxious to prove there was none that she agreed to the test proposed by his father—which was, to drop all money transactions between them for a few months, giving Willie no reason for the change. Grannie, however, being in word and manner, if possible, still kinder to him then ever—and no wonder, seeing she could no more, for the present, let her love out at the pocket hole.

Willie had no anxiety lest he should have displeased her, and soon ceased to think even of the change—except, indeed, sometimes when he wanted a little money very much, and then he would say to himself that he was afraid poor Grannie had been too liberal at first, and had spent all her money upon him. Therefore, he tried to be all the more attentive to her. The result was satisfactory—and the more so that, for all her boasting, his grandmother had not been able to help trembling a little, half with annoyance, half with anxiety, as she let the first few of his services pass without the customary acknowledgment.

"There!" she said one day, at length, triumphantly to Dr. MacMichael. "What do you think of my Willie now? Three months over and gone, and where are your fears? I hope you will trust my judgment a little better after this."

"I'm very glad, anyhow, you put him to the trial," said his father. "It will do him good."

"He wants less of that than most people, Dr. Mac-Michael—present company *not* excepted," said the old lady, rather nettled, but pretending to be more so than she really was.

CHAPTER FIFTEEN
Hydraulics

The first thing Willie did with his room was to put hinges on the windows and make them open, so satisfying his father as to the airiness of the room. Then he began to ask his friends in the village to come and see him in his new quarters. The first who did so was Mrs. Wilson, and Mr. Spelman followed.

But Hector MacAllaster was unwell, and it was a month before he was able to go. But the first day he could he crawled up the hill to the ruins, and then up the winding stair to Willie's nest. The boy was delighted to see him, making him sit in his great armchair and, as the poor man was very tired with the exertion, would have run to the house to get him something. But Hector begged for only a little water, and declared he could take nothing else. Therefore Willie got a tumbler from his dressing table, and went to the other side of the room. Hector, hearing a splashing and rushing, turned around to see. Willie had one hand in a small wooden trough that ran along the wall, and with the other held the tumbler in a stream of water that fell from the side of the trough. When the tumbler was full, the water ceased to overflow. Willie carried the tumbler to Hector, who drank, and said the water was delicious.

Hector could not imagine how the running water had come there, so Willie told him how his grandmother's sovereign and his own hydraulics had brought it about.

Willie had been thinking for some time what a pleasure it would be to have a stream running through his room, and how much labor it would save Tibby. It was no light matter for her old limbs to carry all the water for his bath up that steep narrow winding stair to his room. He reasoned that as the well rose and overflowed when its outlet was stopped, it might rise yet further if it were still confined; for its source was probably the heart of one of the surrounding hills, and water when confined will always rise as high as its source. Therefore, after much meditation as to how it could be accomplished in the simplest and least expensive manner, he set about it.

First of all he cleared away the floor about the well, and built up its circular wall a foot or two higher, with stones picked from those lying about, and with mortar which he made himself. By means of a spirit-level,* he laid the top layer of stones quite level, and introduced into it several blocks of wood instead of stones.

Next he made a small wooden frame, which, by driving spikes between the stones, he fastened to the opening of the underground passage. A well-fitting piece of board could move up and down in it, by means of a projecting handle, and be a more manageable sluice than he had hitherto had.

Then he made a strong wooden lid for the mouth of the well, and screwed it down to the wooden blocks he had built. Through a hole in it, just large enough, came the handle of the sluice.

Next, in the middle of the cover, Willie made a hole with a brace and center bit, and into it drove the end of a strong iron pipe, fitting tight, and long enough to reach almost to the top of the vault. As soon as this was fixed, he shut down the sluice. In a few seconds the water was falling in sheets upon him, and flooding the floor—dashed back from the vault, against which it rushed from the top of the pipe. This was enough for the present, so he raised the sluice and let the water escape again below. It was plain, from the force with which the water struck the vault, that it would yet rise much higher.

Willie scrambled now on the top of the vault, examined the ruins, and soon saw how a pipe brought up through the breach in the vault could be led to the hole in the wall of his room which he had shown his father as a ventilator. But he would not have a closed pipe running through his room, for there would be little good in that. He could have made a hole in it, with a stopper to let the water out when he wanted to use it, but that would be awkward, while all the pleasure lay in seeing the water as it ran. Therefore he got Mr. Spelman to find him a long small pine tree, which he first sawed in two, lengthways, and hollowed into two troughs. Then, by laying the small end of one into the wide end of the other, he had a spout long enough to reach across the room and go through the wall on both sides.

The chief difficulty was to pierce the other wall, for the mortar was very hard. The stones, however, were not very large just there, and with Sandy's help Willie managed it.

The large end of one trough was put through the ventilator hole, and the small end of the other through the hole opposite. Their second ends met in the middle, the one lying into the other, and were supported at the juncture by a prop.

They filled up the two openings around the ends with lime and small stones, making them as tidy as they could, and fitting small slides by which Willie could close up the passages for the water when he pleased. Nothing remained but to solder a lead pipe into the top of the iron one, guide this flexible tube across the ups and downs of the ruins, and lay the end of it into the trough.

At length Willie took his stand at the sluice, and told Sandy to scramble up to the end of the lead pipe, and shout when the water began to pour into the trough. His object was to find how far the sluice required to be shut down in order to send up just as much water as the pipe could deliver. More than that would cause a pressure which might burst their apparatus.

Willie pushed the sluice down a little, and waited a moment. "Is it coming yet, Sandy?" he cried.

"Not a drop!" shouted Sandy.

Willie pushed it a little farther, and then knew by the change in the gurgle below that the water was rising in the well. It soon began to spout from the hole in the cover through which the sluice-handle came up.

"It's coming!" cried Sandy, after a pause. "Not much though."

Down went the sluice a little further still.

"It's pouring," echoed Sandy's voice among the ruins. "As much as ever the pipe can give. Its mouth is quite full."

Willie raised the sluice a little.

"How is it now?" he bawled.

"Less," cried Sandy.

So Willie pushed it back to where it had been last, and made a notch in the handle to know the right place again.

So the water from the Prior's Well went careering through Willie's story-high bedchamber. When he wanted to fill his bath, he had only to stop the run with his hand, and it poured over the sides into it. Tibby was to be henceforth relieved of a great labor, while Willie's eyes were to be delighted with the vision, and his ears with the sounds of the water scampering through his room.

An hour or so after, as he was finishing off something about the mouth of the well, he heard his father calling him.

"Willie! Willie!" he shouted. "Is this any more of your kelpie work?"

"What is it, Father?" cried Willie, as he came bounding to him.

He needed no reply when he saw a great pool of water about the back door, fed by a small stream from the direction of the wood house. Tibby had come out, and was looking on in dismay.

"That's Willie again, sir," she was saying. "You never can tell where he'll be spouting that weary water at you. The whole place 'll be a bog before long, and we'll be all turned into frogs, and have nothing to do but croak. That will be the ruin of us all with cold and coughs."

"You'll be glad enough of it tonight, Tibby," said Willie, laughing prophetically.

"A likely story!" she returned, quite cross. "It'll be into the house if you don't stop it."

"I'll soon do that," said Willie.

Neither he nor Sandy had thought what would become of the water after it had traversed the chamber. There it was pouring down from the end of the wooden spout, just clearing the tarred roof of the spiral stair, and splashing on the ground close to the foot of it. In their eagerness they had never thought of where it would run next. And now Willie was puzzled. Nothing was easier than to stop it for the present, which he did at once—but where was he to send it?

Thinking it over, however, he remembered that just on the other side of the wall was the stable where his father's horses lived, close to the parson's garden—and in the corner, at the foot of the wall, was a drain. All he had to do was to fit another spout to this, at right angles to it, and carry it over the wall.

"You needn't take any water up for me tonight, Tibby," he said, as he went in for supper, for he had already finished his bath.

"Nonsense, Willie," returned Tibby, still out of temper because of the mess at the door. "Your papa says you must have your bath, and my poor old bones must ache for 't."

"The bath's filled already. If you put in one other pailful, it'll run over when I get into it."

"Now, don't you play your tricks with *me,* Willie. I won't

have any more of your joking," returned Tibby.

Nettled at the way she took the information with which he had hoped to please her, he left her to carry up her pail of water—but it was the last, and she thanked him very kindly the next day.

The only remaining question was how to get rid of the bath water. But he soon contrived a sink on the top step of the stair outside the door, which was a little higher than the wall of the stable yard. From there a short pipe was sufficient to carry that water also over into the drain.

Although a severe winter followed, the Prior's Well never froze. And as the pipes were always either empty, or full of running water, they never froze and never burst.

CHAPTER SIXTEEN
A Discovery

The next day after Hector's visit, Willie went to see how he was.

"I certainly am better," Hector said, "and what's more, I've got a strange feeling it was that drink of water you gave me yesterday that has done it. I'm coming up to have some more of it in the evening, if you'll give it to me."

"As much of it as you can drink, Hector, anyhow," said Willie. "You won't drink *my* cow dry."

"I wonder if it could be the water," mused Hector.

"My father says people used to think it cured them. That was some hundred years ago—but if it did so then, I don't see why it shouldn't now. My mother is certainly better, but whether that began since we found the well, I can't be very sure. Tibby is always drinking at it, and she says it does her a world of good."

"I've read somewhere," said the shoemaker, "that wherever there's a hurt there's a help—and when I was a boy, and stung myself with a nettle, I never had far to look for a dock-stalk* with its juice. Who knows but the Prior's Well may be the cure for me? It can't straighten my back, I know, but it may make me stronger for all that, and fitter for the general business."

"I will lay down the pipe for you, if you like, Hector, and then you can drink as much of the water as you please, without asking anybody," said Willie.

Hector laughed. "It's not such a sure thing," he replied, "as

111

to be worth that trouble—and besides, the walk does me good, and a drink once or twice a day is enough—that is, if your people won't think me a trouble, coming so often."

"There's no fear of that," said Willie. "It's our business, you know, to try to cure people. I'll tell you what—couldn't you bring up a bit of your work, and sit in my room sometimes? It's better air there than down here."

"You're very kind, indeed, Willie. We'll see. Meantime, I'll come up morning and evening and have a drink of water, as long at least as the warm weather lasts, and by that time I shall be pretty certain whether it is doing me good or not."

So Hector went on drinking the water and getting a little better.

Next Grannie took to it and, either from imagination, or that it really did her good, declared it was renewing her youth. All the doctor said on the matter was, that the salts it contained could do no one any harm, and might do some people much good; that there was iron in it, which was strengthening, and certain other ingredients which might possibly prevent the iron from interfering with other functions of the system. He said he should not be at all surprised if, someday or other, it regained its old fame as a well of healing.

Mr. Spelman, after a talk with Hector, induced his wife to try it, and she also soon began to think it was doing her good. But beyond these few, no one paid any attention to the Prior's Well or its reborn reputation.

CHAPTER SEVENTEEN

Willie's Sun Scout

Whenever Willie began a new study, he began trying to get at the sense of it. This caused his progress to be slow at first, and him to appear dull among those who merely learned by rote, but as he got a hold of the meaning of it all, his progress grew faster and faster, until at length in most studies he outstripped all the rest.

The constant exercise of his mind through his fingers made it far easier for him to understand the relations of things that go to make up a science. A boy who could put a box together must find Euclid easier than one who had no idea of the practical relations of the boundaries of spaces; one who could contrive a machine like Willie's waterwheel must be able to understand the interdependence of the parts of a sentence better than one equally gifted otherwise, but who did not know how one wheel could move another. Everything he did would help his arithmetic, and geography, and history—and these and those and all things besides, would help him to understand poetry.

In his Latin sentences Willie found the parts dovetailing into each other; finding the terms of equations, he said, was like inventing machines, and he soon grew clever at solving them. It was not from his manual abilities alone that his father gave him the name of "Gutta-Percha Willie," but from the fact that his mind, once warmed to interest, could accommodate itself to the peculiarities of any science, just as the gutta-percha gum which is used for taking a mold fits itself to the outs and ins of any figure.

Willie still employed his waterwheel to pull him out of bed in the middle of the night. He had, of course, to make considerable alterations in and additions to its machinery, after changing his bedroom; for it had then to work in a direction at right angles to the former.

There was something undeniably useful in several of his inventions and many of his efforts. His hydraulics had saved Tibby's aching limbs, his house-building had accommodated Grannie, and for a long time now he had been doing every little repair wanted in the house. If a lock went wrong, he would have it off at once and taken to pieces. If less would not do, he carried it to the smithy, but very seldom troubled Mr. Willett about it. Willie had learned to do small jobs, and to heat and work and temper a piece of iron (within his strength) as well as any man.

His mother did not much like this part of his general apprenticeship, for he would sometimes get his hands so black on Saturday afternoon that he could not get them clean enough for church the next day. And sometimes he would come home with little holes burned here and there in his clothes by the sparks from the red-hot iron beaten on the anvil. Concerning this last evil, she spoke to Hector, who made Willie a leather apron like Mr. Willett's, which he wore thereafter when he had a job to do in the smithy.

But some would regard his other projects as utterly useless. Few would allow there was any value in a waterwheel which could grind no corn, and served only to wake him in the middle of the night—not for work, not for the learning of a single lesson, but only that he might stare out of the window for a while, and then get into bed again. But it *was* a most useful contrivance: all lovely sights tend to keep the soul pure, to lift the heart up to God, and above not only what people call low cares but above what people call reasonable cares—although our great Teacher teaches us that such cares are unjust toward our Father in heaven. More than that, by helping to keep the mind calm and pure, they help to keep the imagination (which is the source of all invention) active, and the judgment (which weighs all its suggestions) just. Whatever is beautiful is of God, and it is only ignorance or a low condition of the heart and soul that does not prize what is beautiful.

Two things together put Willie's next project into his head. He saw a soaring lark radiant with the light of the unrisen sun, and he found in a corner of Spelman's shop a large gilt ball which had belonged to an old clock. The passage in which Spelman had set the clock was so low that he had to remove the ornaments from the top of it—but this one was humbled so that it might be exalted.

The very sight of it set Willie thinking what he could do with it, for he not only meditated how to do a thing, but sometimes what to make a thing do. Before long he set about a huge kite, more than six feet high—a great strong monster, with a tail of portentous length. And to the top of its arch he attached the golden ball. Then he bought a quantity of string, and set his wheel to wake him an hour before sunrise.

One morning was too still, another too cloudy, and a third wet—but at last came one clear and cool, with a steady breeze which sent the leaves of the black poplars all one way. Willie dressed with speed, took his kite and string, and set out for a grass field belonging to Farmer Thomson. He found most of the daisies still buttoned up in sleep, their red tips all together, as tight and close as the lips of a baby that won't take what is offered it—as if they never meant to have anything more to do with the sun, and would never again show him the little golden sun they had inside of them.

In a few minutes the kite had begun to soar, slowly and steadily, then faster and faster, until at length it was towering aloft, tugging and pulling at the string, which Willie could not let out fast enough. He kept looking up after it intently as it rose, when suddenly a new morning star burst out in golden glitter. It was the gilt ball as it saw the sun. The glory which, striking on the heart of the lark, was there transmuted into song, came back from the ball, after its kind, in glow and gleam. Willie danced with delight, and shouted and sang his welcome to the resurrection of the sun, as he watched his golden ball alone in the depth of the air.

He never thought of anyone hearing him, nor was it likely that anyone in the village would be up yet. He was therefore a good deal surprised when he heard the sweet voice of Mona Shepherd behind him. Turning, he saw her running to him bareheaded, with her hair flying in the wind.

"Willie! Willie!" she was crying, half breathless with haste and the buffeting of the breeze.

"Well, Mona, who would have thought of seeing you out so early?"

"Mayn't a girl get up early, as well as a boy? It's not like climbing walls and trees, you know, though I can't see the harm of that either."

"No more can I," said Willie, "if they're not too difficult, you know. But what brought you out now? Do you want me?"

"Mayn't I stop with you? I saw you looking up, and I looked up too, and then I saw something flash, and I dressed as fast as I could, and ran out. Are you catching the lightning?"

"No," said Willie. "Something better than the lightning—the sunlight."

"Is that all?" said Mona, disappointed.

"Why, Mona, isn't the sunlight a better thing than the lightning?" asked philosophical Willie.

"Yes, I dare say, but you can have it any time."

"That only makes it the more valuable. But it's not quite

true when you think of it. You can't have it now, except from my ball."

"Oh, yes, I can!" cried Mona. "There he comes himself!"

And there, to be sure, was the first blinding arc of the sun rising over the eastern hill. Both of them forgot the kite, and turned to watch the great marvel of the heavens, throbbing and pulsing like a sea of flame. When they turned again to the kite they could see the golden ball no longer. Its work was over; it had told them the sun was coming, and now, when the sun was come, it was not wanted anymore. Willie began to draw in his string and roll it up on its stick, slowly pulling down to the earth the soaring sun scout he had sent aloft for the news. He had never flown anything like such a large kite before, and he found it difficult to reclaim.

"Will you take me out with you next time, Willie?" pleaded Mona. "I do so like to be out in the morning, when the wind is blowing, and the clouds are flying about. I wonder why everybody doesn't get up to see the sun rise. Don't you think it is well worth seeing?"

"That I do."

"Then you will let me come with you? I like it so much better when you are with me. Janet spoils it all."

Janet was her old nurse, who seemed to think the main part of her duty was to check Mona's enthusiasm.

"I will," said Willie, "if your papa has no objection."

Mona did not even remember her mama. She had died when Mona was such a little thing.

"Come and ask him, then," said Mona.

So soon as he had secured Sun Scout, as he called his kite with the golden head, she took his hand to lead him to her father.

"He won't be up yet," said Willie.

"Oh, yes, long ago," cried Mona. "He's always up first in the house, and as soon as he's dressed he calls me. He'll be at breakfast by this time, and wondering what could have become of me."

So Willie went with her, and there was Mr. Shepherd, as she had said, already seated at breakfast.

"What have you been about, Mona, my child?" he asked, as soon as he had shaken hands with Willie.

"We've been helping the sun to rise," said Mona, merrily.

"No, no," said Willie. "We've only been having a peep at him in bed, before he got up."

"Oh, yes," chimed in Mona. "And he was fast asleep."

Willie explained the whole matter, and asked if he might call Mona the next time he went out with his kite in the morning.

Mr. Shepherd consented at once, and Mona said he had only to call from his window into their garden, and she would be sure to hear him even if she was asleep.

The next thing Willie did was to construct a small windlass in the garden, with which to wind up or let out the string on the kite. When the next fit morning arrived, Mona and he went out together. As the wind was blowing right through the garden, they did not go to the open field, but sent up the kite from the windlass, and Mona was able by means of the winch to let out the string, while Willie kept watching for the moment when the golden ball should catch the light. They did the same for several mornings after, and Willie managed, with the master's help, to calculate exactly the height at which the ball had flown when first it gained a peep of the sun.

One windy evening they sent the kite up in the hope that it would fly till the morning. But the wind fell in the night, and when the sun came near, there was no golden ball in the air to greet him. So, instead of rejoicing in its glitter far aloft, they had to set out, guided by the string, to find the fallen morning star. The kite was of small consequence, but the golden ball Willie could not replace. Alas! That very evening he had added a great length of string, and when the wind ceased the kite fell into the river. When the searchers finally drew Sun Scout from the water they found his glory had departed: the golden ball had been beaten upon the stones of the stream, and never more did they send him climbing up the heavens to welcome the lord of the day.

Indeed, it was many years before Willie flew a kite again. After a certain conversation with his grandmother, he began to give a good deal more time to his lessons than before. And while his recreations continued to be all of a practical sort, his reading was mostly such as prepared him for college.

CHAPTER EIGHTEEN
A Talk with Grannie

One evening in winter, when Willie had been putting coals on his grannie's fire, she told him to take a chair beside her, as she wanted a little talk with him. He obeyed her gladly.

"Well, Willie," she said, "what would you like to be?"

Willie had just been helping to shoe a horse at the smithy and, in fact, had driven one of the nails—an operation perilous to the horse. Full of the thing which had last occupied him, he answered without a moment's hesitation.

"I should like to be a blacksmith, Grannie."

The old lady smiled. She had seen more black on Willie's hands than could have come from the coals, and judged that he had just come from the smithy.

An unwise grandmother, had she wished to turn him from the notion, would have started an objection at once—probably calling it a dirty trade, or a dangerous trade, or a trade that the son of a professional man could not be allowed to follow. But Willie's grandmother knew better, and went on talking about the thing in the quietest manner.

"It's a fine trade," she said, "thoroughly manly work, and healthy, despite the heat. But why would you take to it, Willie?"

Willie fell back on his principles, and thought for a minute. "Of course, if I'm to be any good at all, I must have a hand in what Hector calls the general business of the universe, Grannie."

"To be sure. And that, as a smith, you would have. But

why should you choose to be a smith rather than anything else in the world?"

"Because people can't get on without horseshoes, and plows and harrows, and tires for cartwheels, and locks, and all that. It would help people very much if I were a smith."

"I don't doubt it. But if you were a mason you could do quite as much to make them comfortable; you could build them houses."

"Yes, I could. It would be delightful to build houses for people. I should like that."

"It's very hard work," said his grandmother. "Only you wouldn't mind that, I know, Willie."

"No man minds hard work," said Willie. "I think I should like to be a mason—for then, you see, I should be able to look at what I had done. The plows and carts would go away out of sight, but the good houses would stand where I had built them, and I should be able to see how comfortable the people were in them. I should come nearer to the people themselves that way with my work. Yes, Grannie, I would rather be a mason than a smith."

"A carpenter fits up the houses inside," said his grandmother. "Don't you think, with his work, he comes nearer the people that live in it than the mason does?"

"To be sure," cried Willie, laughing. "People hardly see the mason's work, except as they're coming up to the door. I know more about carpenter's work too. Yes, Grannie, I *have* settled now. I'll be a carpenter—there!" cried Willie, jumping up from his seat. "If it hadn't been for Mr. Spelman, I don't see how we could have had *you* with us, Grannie. Think of that!"

"Only, if you had been a tailor or a shoemaker, you would have come still nearer to the people themselves."

"I don't know much about tailoring," returned Willie. "I could stitch well enough, but I couldn't cut out. I could soon be a shoemaker, though. I've done everything wanted in a shoe or a boot with my own hands already. Hector will tell you so. I could begin to be a shoemaker tomorrow. That is nearer than a carpenter. Yes."

"I was going to suggest," said his grannie, "that there's a kind of work that goes yet nearer to the people it helps than any of those. But, of course, if you've made up your mind—"

"Oh, no, Grannie! I don't mean it so much as that—if there's a better way, you know. Tell me what it is."

"I want you to think and find out."

Willie thought, looked puzzled, and said he couldn't tell what it was.

"Then you must think a little longer," said his grandmother. "And now go and wash some of that black from your hands."

CHAPTER NINETEEN

A Talk with Mr. Shepherd

In a few minutes Willie came rushing back from his room, with his hands and face half wet and half dry.

"Grannie! Grannie!" he panted. "How can a body be so stupid! Of course you mean a doctor's work! My father comes nearer to people to help them than anybody else can—and yet I never thought what you meant. How is it you can know a thing and not know it at the same time?"

"Well, now you've found what I meant, what do you think of it?" asked his grandmother.

"Why, of course, it's the best of all. When I was a little fellow, I used to think I should be a doctor some day, but I don't feel quite so sure of it now. Do you really think, Grannie, I *could* be a doctor like Papa? That wants such a good head and everything."

"Yes, it does want a good head and everything. But you've got a good enough head to begin with, and it depends on yourself to make it a better one. So long as people's hearts keep growing better, their heads do the same. I think you have every faculty for the making of a good doctor in you."

"Do you really think so, Grannie?" cried Willie, delighted.

"I do, indeed."

"Then I shall ask Papa to teach me."

But Willie did not find his papa so ready to take him in hand. "No, Willie," he said. "You must learn a great many other things before it would be of much use for me to commence my part. I will teach you, if you like, after school

125

hours, to compound certain medicines—but the important thing is to get on at school. You are quite old enough now to work at home too, and though I don't want to confine you to your lessons, I should like you to spend a couple of hours at them every evening. You can have the remainders of the evenings, all the mornings before breakfast, and the greater parts of your half-holidays for whatever you like to do of another sort."

Willie never required any urging to do what his father wished. He became at once more of a student, without becoming much less of a workman. He found plenty of time to do all he wanted, by being more careful of his odd moments.

One lovely evening in spring, the sun had gone down and left the air soft and balmy and full of the scents which rise from the earth after a shower, and full as well of the odors of the buds which were swelling and bursting in all directions. Willie was standing looking out of his open window into the parson's garden, when Mr. Shepherd saw him and called to him.

"Come down here, Willie," he said. "I want to have a little talk with you."

Willie got on the wall from the top of his stair, dropped into the stable yard, which served for the parson's pony as well as the doctor's two horses, and then passed into Mr. Shepherd's garden, where the two began to walk up and down together.

The year was like a child waking up from a sleep into which he had fallen crying. Its life was returning to it, fresh and new. It was as if God were again drawing nigh to His world. All the winter through He had never left it, only had, as it were, been rolling it along the path before Him—but now He had taken it up in His hand, and was carrying it for a while. And that was how its birds were singing so sweetly, and its buds were coming so blithely out-of-doors. The wind blew so soft, and the rain fell so repentantly, and the earth sent up such a gracious odor.

"The year is coming to itself again, Willie—growing busy once more," Mr. Shepherd said.

"Yes," answered Willie. "It's been all but dead, and has come to life again. It must have had the Doctor to it."

"Eh? What doctor, Willie?"

"Well, you know, there is but One that could be doctor to this big world."

"Yes, surely," returned Mr. Shepherd. "And that brings me to what I wanted to talk to you about. I hear your father means to make a doctor of you."

"Yes. Isn't it good of him?" said Willie.

"Then you would like it?"

"Yes, that I should!"

"Why would you like it?"

"Because I *must* have a hand in the general business."

"What do you mean by that?"

Willie set forth Hector MacAllaster's way of thinking about such matters.

"Very good—very good, indeed!" remarked Mr. Shepherd. "But why, then, should you prefer being a doctor to being a shoemaker? Is it because you will get better paid for it?"

"I never thought of that," returned Willie. "Of course I should be better paid—for Hector couldn't keep a horse, and a horse I must have, else some of my patients would be dead before I could get to them. But that's not why I want to be a doctor. It's because I want to help people."

"What makes you want to help people?"

"Because it's the best thing you can do with yourself."

"Who told you that?"

"I don't know. It seems as if everybody and everything has been teaching me that, ever since I can remember."

"Well, it's no wonder it should seem as if everything taught you that. It is what God is always doing—and what

Jesus taught us as the law of His kingdom—which is the only real kingdom—namely, that the greatest man in it is he who gives himself the most to help other people. It was because Jesus Himself did so—giving Himself up utterly—that God so highly exalted Him and gave Him a name above every name. And, indeed, if you are a good doctor, you will be doing something of what Jesus did when He was in the world."

"Yes, but He didn't give people medicine to cure them."

"No, that wasn't necessary, because He was Himself the cure. But now that He is not present with His bodily presence, medicine and advice and other good things are just the packets in which He wraps up the healing He sends. And the wisest doctor is but the messenger who carries to the sick as much of healing and help as the great Doctor sees fit to send. For He is so anxious to cure thoroughly that in many cases He will not cure all at once."

"How I *should* like to take His healing about!" cried Willie. "Just as the doctor's boys take the medicines about in baskets—Grannie tells me they do in big towns. I *should* like to be the Great Doctor's boy!"

"You really think then," Mr. Shepherd resumed, after a pause, "that a doctor's is the best way of helping people?"

"Yes, I do," answered Willie, decidedly. "A doctor, you see, comes nearest to them with his help. It's not the outside of a man's body he helps, but his inside health—how he feels, you know."

Mr. Shepherd again thought for a few moments, and said, "What's the difference between your father's work and mine?"

"I must think before I can answer that," said Willie. "It's not so easy to put things in words! You very often go to help the same people: that's something to start with."

"But not to give them the same help."

"No, not quite. And yet—"

"At least, I cannot write prescriptions or compound medicines for them, seeing I know nothing about such things," said Mr. Shepherd. "But, on the other hand, though I can't give them medicine out of your papa's basket, your papa very often gives them medicine out of mine."

"That's a riddle, I suppose," said Willie.

"No, it's not. How is it your papa can come so near people to help them?"

"He gives them things that make them well again."

"What do they do with the things he gives them?"

"They take them."

"How?"

"Put them in their mouths and swallow them."

"Couldn't they take them at their ears?"

"No," answered Willie, laughing.

"Why not?"

"Because their ears aren't meant for taking them."

"Aren't their ears meant for taking anything, then?"

"Only words."

"Well, if one were to try, mightn't words be mixed so as to be medicine?"

"I don't see how."

"If you were to take a few strong words, a few persuasive words, and a few tender words, mightn't you mix them so— that is, so set them in order—as to make them a good medicine for a sore heart, for instance?"

"Ah! I see! Yes, the medicine for the heart must go in at the ears."

"Not necessarily. It might go in at the eyes. Jesus gave it at the eyes, for doubting hearts, when He said, 'Consider the lilies—consider the ravens.'"

"At the ears too, though," said Willie. "Just as Papa sometimes gives medicine to be taken and to be rubbed both."

"Only the ears could have done nothing with the words if the eyes hadn't taken in the things themselves first. But where does this medicine go to, Willie?"

"I suppose it must go to the heart, if that's the place that wants healing."

"Does it go to what a doctor would call the heart, then?"

"No, it must go to what a clergyman—to what *you* call the heart."

"And which heart is nearer to the person himself?"

Willie thought for a moment, then answered merrily, "Why, the doctor's heart, to be sure!"

"No, Willie. You're wrong there," said Mr. Shepherd, looking, as he felt, a little disappointed.

"Oh yes, please!" said Willie. "I'm almost sure I'm right this time."

"No, Willie. What the clergyman calls the heart is the nearest to the man himself."

"No, no," persisted Willie. "The heart you've got to do with *is* the man himself. So of course the doctor's heart is the nearer to the man."

Mr. Shepherd laughed a low, pleasant laugh. "You're quite right, Willie. You've got the best of it. I'm very pleased. But then, Willie, doesn't it strike you that after all there might be a closer way of helping men than the doctor's way?"

Again Willie thought a while. "There would be," he said, "if you could give them medicine to make them happy when they are miserable."

"Even the doctor can do a little of that," returned Mr. Shepherd, "for people are much happier in good health than when they are ill."

"If you could give them what would make them good when they are bad then," said Willie.

"Ah, there you have it!" rejoined Mr. Shepherd. "That *is* the very closest way of helping men."

"But nobody can do that. Nobody but God can make a bad man good," said Willie.

"Certainly. But He uses medicines, and He sends people

about with them, just like the doctors' boys you were speaking of. What else am *I* here for? I've been carrying His medicines about for a good many years now."

"Then *your* work and not my father's comes nearest to people to help them after all! My father's work, I see, doesn't help the very man himself. It only helps his body, or at best his happiness. It doesn't go deep enough to touch himself. But yours helps the very man. Yours is the best after all."

"I don't know," returned Mr. Shepherd, thoughtfully. "It depends, I think, on the kind of preparations gone through."

"Oh yes!" said Willie. "You had to go through the theological classes. I must of course take the medical."

"That's true, but it's not true enough," said Mr. Shepherd. "That wouldn't make a fraction of the difference I mean. There's just one preparation essential for a man who would carry about the best sort of medicines. Can you think what it is? It's not necessary for the other sort."

"The man must be good," said Willie. "I suppose that's it."

"That doesn't make the difference exactly," returned Mr. Shepherd. "It is as necessary for a doctor to be good as for a parson."

"Yes," said Willie, "but though the doctor were a bad man, his medicines might be good."

"Not by any means so likely to be!" said the parson. "You can never be sure that anything a bad man has to do with will be good. It may be, because no man is all bad—but you can't be sure of it. We are coming nearer it now. Mightn't the parson's medicines be good if he were bad, just as well as the doctor's?"

"Less likely still, I think," said Willie. "The words might be all of the right sort, but they would be like medicines that had lain in a drawer or stood in a bottle till the good was out of them."

"You're coming very near to the difference of preparation I wanted to point out to you," said Mr. Shepherd. "It is this:

that the physician of men's selves, commonly called souls, must have taken and must keep taking the medicine he carries about with him—while the less the doctor wants of his own the better."

"I see, I see," cried Willie, whom a fitting phrase or figure or form of expressing a thing pleased as much as a clever machine. "I see! It's all right. I understand now."

"But," Mr. Shepherd went on, "your father carries about both sorts of medicines in his basket. He is such a healthy man that I believe he very seldom uses any of his own medicines. But he is always taking some of the other sort, and that's what makes him fit to carry them about. He does far more good among the sick than I can. Many who don't like my medicine, will yet take a little of it when your father mixes it with his, as he has a wonderful art in doing. I hope, when your turn comes, you will be able to help the very man himself, as your father does."

"Do you want me to be a doctor of *your* kind, Mr. Shepherd?"

"No. It would be a very wrong thing to take up that basket without being told by Him who makes the medicine. If He wants a man to do so, He will let him know—He will call him and tell him to do it. But everybody ought to take the medicine, for everybody needs it; and the happy thing is, that as soon as anyone has found how good it is—food and wine and all upholding things in one—he becomes both able and anxious to give it to others. If you would help people as much as your father does, you must begin by taking some of the real medicine yourself."

This conversation gave Willie a good deal to think about. And he had much need to think about it, for soon after this he left his father's house for the first time in his life, and went to a great town, to receive there a little further preparation for college. The next year he gained a scholarship or, as they call it there, a bursary, and was at once fully occupied with classics and mathematics. He hoped, however, to combine with them the next year certain scientific studies bearing less indirectly upon the duties of the medical man.

CHAPTER TWENTY
Agnes Wishes

During the time he was at college, Willie often thought of what Mr. Shepherd had said to him. When he was tempted to any self-indulgence, the thought would always arise that this was not the way to become able to help people, especially the real selves of them; and, when among the medical students, he could not help thinking how much better doctors some of them would make if they would but try the medicine of the other basket for themselves. Willie thought this especially when he saw that they cared nothing for their patients, and had no desire to take a part in the general business for the work's sake, but only wanted a practice that they might make a living. For such are nearly as unfit to be healers of the body as mere professional clergymen are to be healers of broken hearts and wounded minds. To do a man good in any way, you must sympathize with him—to know what he feels, and reflect the feeling in your own mirror. And to be a good doctor, one must love to heal; must honor the art of the physician and rejoice in it; must give himself to it, that he may learn all of it that he can, from its root of love to its branches of theory, and its leaves and fruits of healing.

Willie always came home to Priory Leas for the summer intervals, when you may be sure there was great rejoicing—loudest on the part of Agnes, who was then his constant companion—at least, as much as she was allowed. Willie saw a good deal of Mona Shepherd also, who had long been set free from the oppressive charge of Janet, and was now under the care of a governess, a wise, elderly lady. As the governess was a great friend of Mrs. MacMichael, the two families were even more together now than in former years.

Of course, while Willie was at college he had no time to work with his hands: all his labor there had to be with his head. But when he came home he had plenty of time for both sorts. He spent a couple of hours before breakfast in the study of physiology; after breakfast, another hour or two either in the surgery, or in a part of the ruins which he had roughly fitted up for a laboratory with a bench, a few shelves, and a furnace.

His father, however, did not favor his being in the furnace for a long time together, for young experimenters are commonly careless, and will often neglect proper precautions— breathing, for instance, many gases they ought not to breathe. Willie was so careful over Agnes, however, that often he would not let her in at all, and when he did, he generally confined himself to her amusement. He showed her such lovely things! Liquids that changed from one gorgeous hue to another; bubbles that burst into flame, and ascended in rings of white revolving smoke; light so intense that it seemed to darken the daylight. Sometimes Mona would be of the party, and nothing pleased Agnes or her better than such wonderful things as these. Willie found it amusing to hear Agnes, who was sharp enough to pick up the chemical names, dropping the big words from her lips— *phosphuretted hydrogen, metaphosphoric acid, sesqui-ferrocyanide of iron,* and such.

Then he would give an hour to preparation for the studies of his next college term; after that, until dinner, he would work at his bench or lathe, generally at something for his mother or grandmother; or he would do a little mason work among the ruins, patching and strengthening, or even buttressing where he thought there was the most danger of further fall. He had resolved that, if he could help it, not another stone should tumble to the ground.

In this, Willie's first summer at home from college, he also fitted up a small forge—in a part of the ruins where there was a wide chimney, whose vent ran up a long way unbroken. Here he constructed a pair of great bellows, and set up an old anvil, which he bought for a trifle from Mr. Willett. Here his father actually trusted him to shoe his horses—nor did he ever find a nail of Willie's driving ever need drawing before the shoe had to give place to a new one.

In the afternoon, Willie always read history or tales or poetry, and in the evening he did whatever he felt inclined to do. One such lovely evening in June, he came upon Agnes (who was now eight years old) lying under the largest elm of a clump of great elms and Scotch firs at the bottom of the garden. They were the highest trees in all the neighborhood, and his father was very fond of them. To look up into those elms in the summertime your eyes seemed to lose their way in a mist of leaves; whereas the firs had only great, bony, bare, gaunt arms, with a tuft of bristles here and there. But when a ray of the setting sun alighted upon one of these firs it shone like a flamingo. It seemed as if the surly old tree and the gracious sunset had some secret between them, which, as often as they met, broke out in ruddy flame.

Now Agnes was lying on the thin grass under this clump of trees, looking up into their mystery. She was sucking her thumb—her custom always when she was thoughtful, and thoughtful she seemed now, for the tears were in her eyes.

"What is the matter with my pet?" asked Willie.

But instead of jumping up and flinging her arms about him, she only looked at him, gave a little sigh, drew her thumb from her mouth, pointed with it up into the tree, and said, "I can't get up there! I wish I were a bird," and put her thumb in her mouth again.

"But if you were a bird, you wouldn't be a girl, you know,

and you wouldn't like that," said Willie. "At least *I* shouldn't like it."

"*I* shouldn't mind. I would rather have wings and fly about in the trees."

"If you had wings you couldn't have arms."

"I'd rather have wings."

"If you were a bird up there, you would be sure to wish you were a girl down here. For if you were a bird you couldn't lie in the grass and look up into the tree."

"Oh, yes, I could."

"What a comical little bird you would look then—lying on your round feathery back, with wings spread out to keep you from rolling over, and little sparkling eyes, one on each side of such a long beak, staring up into the tree!"

"But *wouldn't* it be nice," persisted Agnes, "to be so tall as the birds can make themselves with their wings? Fancy having your head up there in the green leaves—so cool! And hearing them all whisper, whisper, about your ears, and being able to look down on people's heads, you know, Willie! I do wish I were a bird! I do!"

But with Willie to comfort and play with her, she soon forgot her soaring ambition. Willie, however, did not forget. If Agnes wished to enjoy the privacy of the leaves up in the height of the trees, why shouldn't she, if he could help her to do it? Certainly he couldn't change her arms into wings, or cover her with feathers, or make her bones hollow so that the air might get all through her, even into her quills—but he could get her up into the tree, and even something more, perhaps. He would think about it, for how it was to be done he did not yet see.

Almost the moment he had arrived home, Willie had set his wheel in order. And now more than ever he enjoyed being pulled out of bed in the middle of the night, especially in fine weather. Then, in that hushed hour when the night is just melting into the morn, and the earth looks as if she were losing her dreams, yet had not begun to recognize her own thoughts, he would frequently go out into the garden, and wander about for a few thoughtful minutes.

The same night, when his wheel pulled him, Willie rose and went out into the garden. The night was at odds with morning which was which. An occasional bat would flit like a doubtful shadow across his eyes, but a cold breath of air was roaming about as well, which was not of the night at all, but plainly belonged to the morning. Willie wandered to the bottom of the garden—to the clump of trees, lay down where Agnes had been lying the night before, and thought until he felt in himself how the child had felt when she longed to be a bird. What could he do to content her? He knew every bough of the old trees himself, having scrambled ove₁ them like a squirrel scores of times; but even if he could get Agnes up the bare pole of an elm or fir, he could not trust her to go scrambling about the branches. On the other hand, wherever he could go, he could surely help Agnes to go. Having gathered a thought or two, he went back to bed.

The very next evening he set to work, and spent the whole of that and the following at his bench—planing and shaping and generally preparing for construction of the plan which he now had clearly in his head. On the third evening he carried half a dozen long poles, and wheeled several barrowfuls of short planks, measuring but a few inches over two feet, down to the clump of trees.

At the foot of the largest elm he began to dig, with the intention of inserting the thick end of one set of poles—but he soon found it impossible to get half deep enough, because of the tremendous roots of the tree. Giving it up, he thought of a better plan.

He set off to the smithy, and bought from Mr. Willett some fifteen feet of iron rod, with a dozen staples. Carrying them home to his small forge, Willie cut the rod into equal lengths of a little over two feet, and made a hook at both ends of each length. Then he carried them down to the elm, and drove six of the staples into the bole of the tree at equal distances all round it, a foot from the ground. The other staples he drove into the six poles, a foot from the thick end. Then he connected the poles with the tree, each by a hooked rod and its corresponding staples, so the tops of the poles just reached to the first fork of the elm. Then he nailed a bracket to the tree, at the height of an easy step from the ground, and at the same height nailed a piece of wood across between two of the poles. Resting on the bracket and this piece of wood, he laid the first step of a stair, and fastened it firmly to both. Another bracket a little higher, and another piece of wood nailed to two poles raised the next step—and so he went round and round the tree in an ascending spiral, climbing on the steps already placed to fix others above them. Encircling the tree some four or five times (for he wanted the ascent easy for little feet), he reached the first fork. There he laid a platform or landing, and paused to consider what to do next. All this he had done by the third evening from the laying of the first step.

From the fork many boughs rose and spread—among them two very near each other, between which he saw how he might build a little straight staircase leading up into a perfect wilderness of leaves and branches. Although he found it more difficult than he had expected, he soon suc-ceeded in building a safe stair between the boughs, with a handrail of rope on each side.

But Willie had chosen to ascend in this direction for another reason as well: one of these boughs was in close contact with a bough belonging to one of the largest red firs. On this fir bough he constructed a landing-place, upon which it was as easy as possible to step from the stair in the elm. Next he laid along the bough a plank steadied by blocks underneath—a level for little feet. Then he began to weave a network of rope and string along each side of the bough, so that the child could not fall off. But he found this rather a long job, and thought it a pity to balk her of so much pleasure merely for the sake of surprising her the more thoroughly, so he resolved to reveal what he had already done, and permit her to enjoy it.

Willie had taken Mona into his confidence, and she had kept Agnes out of the way now for nearly a whole week of evenings. But Mona was finding it more and more difficult to restrain her from rushing off in search of Willie, and was very glad indeed when he told her that he was not going to keep the thing a secret any longer.

CHAPTER TWENTY-ONE

Agnes the Bird

But Willie began to think he might give Agnes two surprises out of it, with a dream into the bargain.

She always went to bed at seven o'clock, so that by the time the other people in the house began to think of retiring, she was generally fast asleep. About ten o'clock, therefore, the next night, just as a great round moon was peering above the horizon, with a quantity of mackerel clouds ready to receive her when she rose a yard or two higher, Willie took a soft shawl of his mother's and went into Agnes' room. Having wrapped her in the shawl, with a corner of it over her head and face, he carried her out into the garden, down to the trees, and up the stair into the midst of the great boughs and branches of the elm tree.

It was a very warm night, with a soft breath of south wind blowing, and there was no risk of her taking cold. He uncovered her face, but did not wake her, leaving that to the change of her position and the freshness of the air. Nor was he disappointed. In a few moments she began to stir, then half-opened her eyes, then shut them, then opened them again, then rubbed them, then drew a deep breath, and then began to lift her head from Willie's shoulder, and look about her. Through the thick leaves the moon was shining like a great white fire, and must have looked to her sleepy eyes almost within a yard of her. Even if she had not been half asleep, so beheld through the trees, it would have taken her a while to make up her mind what the huge bright thing was.

Then she heard a great fluttering as if the leaves were talking to her, and out of them came a soft wind that blew in her face, and felt very sweet and pleasant. She rubbed her eyes again, but could not get the sleep out of them. At last she said to Willie, who stood as still as a stone—but her tongue and her voice and her lips could hardly make the words she wanted them to utter.

"Am I awake? Am I dreaming? It's so nice!"

Willie did not answer her, and the little head sunk on his shoulder again. He drew the corner of the shawl over it, and carried her back to her bed. When he laid her down, she opened her eyes wide, stared him in the face for a moment, as if she knew all about everything except just what she was looking at, put her thumb in her mouth, and was fast asleep.

The next morning at breakfast, her papa out, and her mamma not yet come down, she told Willie that she had had such a beautiful dream! That an angel with great red wings came and took her in his arms, and flew up and up with her to a cloud that lay close by the moon. The cloud was made all of little birds that kept fluttering their wings and talking to each other, and the fluttering of their wings made a wind in her face, and the wind made her very happy. The moon kept looking through the birds quite close to them, and smiling at her, and she saw the face of the man in the moon quite plainly. But then it grew dark and began to thunder, and the angel went down very fast, and the thunder was the clapping of his big red wings, and he flew with her into mamma's room, and laid her down in her bed, and when she looked at him he was so like Willie!

"Do you think the dream could have come of your wishing to be a bird, Agnes?" asked Willie.

"I don't know. Perhaps," replied Agnes. "Are you angry with me for wishing I was a bird, Willie?"

"No, darling. What makes you ask such a question?"

"Because ever since then you won't let me go with you—

when you are doing things, you know."

"Why, you were in the laboratory with me yesterday!" said Willie.

"Yes, but you wouldn't have me in the evening when you used to let me be with you always. What are you doing down among the trees *always* now?"

"If you will have patience and not go near them all day, I will show you in the evening."

Agnes promised, and Willie gave the whole day to finishing things a bit. Among other things he wove such a network along the bough of the Scotch fir, that it was quite safe for Agnes to walk on it down to the great red bole of the tree. There he was content to pause for the present, after constructing a little chair of bough and branch and rope and twig in which she could safely sit.

Just as he had finished the chair, he heard her voice calling, in a tone that grew more and more pitiful, "Willie! Willie! Willie! Willie!"

He got down and ran to find her. She was at the window of his room, where she had gone to wait till he called her, but her patience had at last given way.

"I'm *so* tired, Willie! Mayn't I come yet?"

"Wait just one moment more," said Willie, and ran to the house for his mother's shawl.

As soon as he began to wrap it about her, Agnes said thoughtfully, "Somebody did that to me before—not long ago. I remember! It was the angel in my dream!"

When Willie put the corner over her face, she said, "He did that too!" and when he took her in his arms, she said, "He did that too! How funny you should do just what the angel did in my dream!"

Willie ran about with her here and there through the ruins, into the house, up and down the stairs, and through the garden in many directions, until he was satisfied he must have thoroughly bewildered her as to where they were, and then at last sped with her up the stair to the fork of the elm tree. There he threw back the shawl and told her to look.

To see her first utterly bewildered expression—then the slow glimmering dawn of intelligence, as she began to understand where she was—next the gradual rise of light in her face as if it came there from some spring down below, until it broke out in a smile all over it, when she realized that this was what he had been working at, and why he wouldn't have her with him—gave Willie all the pleasure he had hoped for. It quite satisfied him, and made him count his labor well rewarded.

"O Willie, Willie! It was all for me! Wasn't it, now?"

"Yes, it was, pet," said Willie.

"It was all to make a bird of me, wasn't it?" she went on.

"Yes, as much of a bird as I could. I couldn't give you wings, you know, and I hadn't any of my own to fly up with you to the moon, as the angel in your dream did. The dream was much nicer, wasn't it?"

"I'm not sure about that—really I'm not. I think it is nicer to have a wind coming you don't know from where, and making all the leaves flutter about, than to have the wings of birdies making the wind. And I don't care about the man in the moon so much. He's not so nice as you, Willie. And the red ray of the sun through there on the fir tree is as good nearly as the moon."

"Oh! But you may have the moon, if you wait a bit. She'll be too late tonight, though."

"But now I think of it, Willie," said Agnes, "I do believe it wasn't a dream at all."

"Do you think a real angel carried you really up to the moon, then?" asked Willie.

"No, but a real Willie carried me really up into this tree, and the moon shone through the leaves, and I thought they were birds. You're my angel, Willie, only better to me than twenty hundred angels."

And Agnes threw her arms round his neck, and hugged and kissed him.

As soon as he could speak, that is, as soon as she ceased choking him, he said, "You *were* up in this tree last night, and the leaves were fluttering the leaves, and the moon was shining through them—"

"And you carried me in this shawl, and that was the red wings of the angel," cried Agnes, dancing with delight.

"Yes, pet, I daresay it was. But aren't you sorry to lose your big angel?"

"The angel was only in a dream, and you're here, Willie. Besides, you'll be a big angel someday, and then you'll have wings, and be able to fly me about."

"But you'll have wings of your own then, and be able to fly with me."

"But I *may* fold them up sometimes—mayn't I? For it would be much nicer to be carried by *your* wings—sometimes, you know. Look, look, Willie! Look at the sunbeam on the trunk of the fir—how red it's got. I do wish I could have a peep at the sun. Where can he be? I should see him if I were to go into his beam there, shouldn't I?"

"He's shining past the end of the cottage," said Willie. "Go, and you'll see him."

"Go where?" asked Agnes.

"Into the red sunbeam on the fir tree."

"I haven't got my wings yet, Willie."

"That's what people very often say when they're not inclined to try what they can do with their legs."

"But I can't go there, Willie."

"You haven't tried."

"How am I to try?"

"You're not even trying to try. You're standing talking, and saying you can't."

It was nearly all Agnes could do to keep from crying. But

she felt she must do something more lest Willie should be vexed. There seemed but one way to get nearer the sunbeam, and that was to go down this tree and run to the foot of the other. What if Willie had made a stair up it also? But as she turned she caught sight of the straight staircase between the two boughs, and with a shriek of delight, up she ran. At the end of the stairs she sprang upon the bough of the fir, and in a moment more was sitting in the full light of the sunset.

"O Willie, Willie! This *is* grand! How good, how kind of you! You *have* made a bird of me! What will Papa and Mamma say? Won't they be delighted? I must run and fetch Mona."

Agnes hurried across again, and down the stair, and away to look for Mona Shepherd, shouting with delight as she ran. In a few minutes her cries had gathered the whole house to the bottom of the garden, as well as Mr. Shepherd and Mona and Mrs. Hunter. Dr. MacMichael and all of them went up into the tree. Mr. Shepherd came last, and with some misgivings; having no mechanical faculty himself, he could not rightly value Willie's, and feared that he might not have made the stair safe. But Dr. MacMichael soon satisfied him, showing him how strong and firm Willie had made every part of it.

The next evening, Willie went on with his plan, which was to make a way for Bird Agnes from one tree to another over the whole of the clump. It took him many evenings to complete it, and a good many more to construct in the elm tree a thin wooden house perched upon several of the strongest boughs and branches. He called it Bird Agnes' Nest. It had doors and windows, and several stories in it, though the upper stories did not rest on the lower, but upon higher branches of the tree. To two of these branches he made stairs, and a rope-ladder to a third. When the house was finished, he put a little table in the largest room, and having carried some light chairs from the house, asked his father and mother and grandmother to tea in Bird Agnes' Nest.

But Grannie declined to go up the tree. She said *her* climbing days were over long ago.

CHAPTER TWENTY-TWO
Willie's Plans Bud

But either Grannie's climbing days were over, or were only beginning. The next winter, while Willie was at college, Grannie was taken ill—and although they sent for him to come home at once, she had climbed higher before he arrived. When they opened her will, they found that she had left everything to Willie. There was more than a hundred pounds in ready money, and property that brought in about fifty pounds a year—not much to one who would have spent everything on himself, but a good deal to one who loved other people, and for their sakes would contrive that a little should go a long way.

So Willie was able to relieve his father by paying all his own college expenses. He saved a little too, as his father wished, until he should see how best to use it. His father always talked about *using,* never about *spending* money.

When Willie came home the next summer, he moved again into his old room, for Agnes slept in a little closet off her mother's, and much preferred that to a larger and more solitary room for herself. His mother especially was glad to have him under the same roof once more at night. But Willie felt that something ought to be done with the room he had left in the ruins, for nothing ought to be allowed to spoil by uselessness. He did not, however, see to what use he could turn it.

No day passed while he was at home without his going to see Mr. Willett or Mr. Spelman or Mrs. Wilson. Willie went to see Hector the most often of all, he being his favorite, and sickly, and therefore in most need of attention. But he greatly improved his acquaintance with William Webster; and although he had now so much to occupy him, would not be satisfied until he was able to drive the shuttle, and work the treadles and the batten, and, in short, turn out almost as good a bit of linen as William himself—only he needed about twice as much time to do it.

One day, going in to see Hector, Willie found him in bed and very poorly.

"My shoemaking is nearly over, Mr. Willie," he said. "But I don't mind much. I'm sure to find a corner in the general business ready for me somewhere when I'm not wanted here anymore."

"Have you been drinking the water lately?" asked Willie.

"No. I was very busy last week, and hadn't time, and it was rather cold for me to go out. But for that matter the wind blew in through door and window so dreadfully, and it's but a clay floor, and firing is dear. I caught a cold, and a cold is. the worst thing for me—that is, for this poor rickety body of mine—and this cold is a bad one."

Here a great fit of coughing came on, accompanied by symptoms that Willie saw were dangerous, and he went home at once to get him some medicine.

On the way back a thought struck him. However, he said nothing to Hector until he talked to his father and mother that same evening at supper.

"I'll tell you what, Hector," Willie said, when he went to see him the next day. "You must come and occupy my room in the ruins. Since Grannie died I don't want it, and it's a pity to have it lying idle. It's a deal warmer than this, and I'll have to get a stove in before winter. You won't have to work so hard when you've got no rent to pay, and you will have as much of the water as you like without the trouble of walking up the hill for it. Then there's the garden for you to walk in when you please—all on a level, and only the little stair to climb to get back to your own room."

"But I should be such a trouble to you all, Mr. Willie!"

"You'd be no trouble—we've two servants now. If you like you can give the little one a shilling now and then, and she'll be glad enough to make your bed, and sweep out your room. And you know Tibby has a great regard for you, and will be very glad to do all the cooking you want—it's not much, I know: your porridge and a cup of tea is about all. And then there's my father to look after your health, and Agnes to amuse you sometimes, and my mother to look after everything, and—"

Here poor Hector fairly broke down. When he recovered himself he said, "But how could gentle folks like you bear to see a hump-backed creature like me crawling about the place?"

"They would only enjoy it the more that you enjoyed it," said Willie.

It was all arranged. As soon as Hector was able to be moved, he was carried up to the Ruins, and there nursed by everybody. Nothing could exceed his comfort now but his gratitude. He was soon able to work again, and as he was evidently happier when doing a little toward the general business, Dr. MacMichael thought it best for him.

One day Willie was at work in his laboratory, and half-stifled himself with a sudden fume of chlorine. He opened the door for some air just as Hector passed it. Willie stood at the door and followed him down the walk with his eyes, watching him as he went—now disappearing behind the blossoms of an apple tree, now climbing one of the little mounds, and now getting up into the elm tree and looking about him on all sides, his sickly face absolutely shining with pleasure.

But, thought Willie, *why should Hector be the only invalid to have this pleasure? And what if this is what my Grannie's money was given me for?*

That night Willie had a dream. He dreamed that he was pulled up in the middle of the night by his wheel, and went down to go into the garden. But the moment he was out of the back door, he fancied there was something strange going on in his room in the ruins. When he climbed the stairs and opened the door, there was Hector MacAllaster where he ought to be, asleep in his bed. But there *was* something strange going on: a stream, which came dashing over the side of the wooden spout, was flowing all round Hector's bed, and then away he knew not where. And in the far wall was a door which was new to him. He opened it, and found himself in another chamber, like his own—and there also lay someone, he knew not who, in a bed, with a stream of water flowing all about it. There was also a second door, beyond which was a third room, and a third patient asleep, and a third stream flowing around the bed, and a third door beyond. He went from room to room, on and on, through about a hundred such, he thought, and at length came to a vaulted chamber which seemed to be over the well.

From the center of the vault rose a great chimney, and under the chimney was a huge fire, and on the fire stood a mighty golden cauldron, up to which, through a large pipe, came the water of the well, and went pouring in with a great rushing, and hissing, and bubbling. From the other side of the cauldron the water rushed away through another pipe into the trough that ran through all the chambers, and made the rivers that flowed past the beds of the sleeping patients. And by the fire stood two angels who made a great fanning with their grand lovely wings, and so blew the fire up loud and strong about the golden cauldron. And when Willie looked into their faces, he saw that one of them was his father, and the other Mr. Shepherd. And he gave a great cry of delight, and woke weeping.

CHAPTER TWENTY-THREE

Willie's Plans Blossom

In the morning, Willie's head was full of his dream. How gladly would he have turned it into a reality! That was impossible—but might he not do something toward it?

He had long ago seen that those who are doomed not to realize their ideal, are just those who will not take the first step toward it. They think and they say that they would give their life for it, and yet they will not give a single hearty effort. Hence they just stop where they are, or rather go back and back until they do not care a bit for the thoughts they used to think so great that they cherished them for the glory of having thought them. But even the wretched people who set their hearts on making money, begin by saving the first penny they can, and then the next and the next. And they have their reward: they get the riches they want—with the loss of their souls to be sure, but that they did not think of. The people on the other hand who want to be noble and good, begin by taking the first thing that comes to their hand and doing that right, and so they go on from one thing to another, growing better and better.

In the same way, although it would have been absurd for Willie to rack his brain for some scheme by which to restore such a grand building as the Priory, he could yet see that the hundredth room did not come next to the first, neither did the third; the one after the first was the second, and he might do something toward the existence of that.

He went out immediately after breakfast, and began

peering about the ruins to see where the second room might be. To his delight he saw that, with a little contrivance, it could be built on the other side of the wall of Hector's room.

He had plenty of money for it. He thought it all over himself, talked it all over with his father, and then consulted Spelman. The end was, that without spending his little store, he had, before the time came for his return to the college, built another room. As the garret was full of his grandmother's furniture, nothing was easier than to fit it up—and that very nicely too. It remained only to find an occupant for it.

This would have been easy enough also without going far from the door, but both Willie and his father were practical men, and therefore could not be content with merely doing good: they wanted to do as much good as they could. It would not therefore satisfy them to put into their new room such a person as Mrs. Wilson, who could get on pretty well where she was, though she might have been made more comfortable. But suppose they could find the sickly mother of a large family, whom a few weeks of change, with the fine air from the hills and the wonderful water from the Prior's Well, would restore to strength and cheerfulness? How much more good would they not be doing in that way— seeing that to help a mother with children is to help all the children as well, not to mention the husband and the friends of the family! There were plenty such to be found among the patients Willie attended while at college. The expense of living was not great at Priory Leas, and Dr. MacMichael was willing to bear that, if only to test the influences of the water and climate upon strangers.

Although it was not the best season for the experiment, it was yet successful with the pale rheumatic mother of six, whom Willie first sent home to his father's care. She returned to her children at Christmas, comparatively a hale woman, capable of making them and everybody about her twice as happy as before. Another like her took her place, with like result—and before long the healing that hovered about Priory Leas began to be known and talked of among the professors of the college and the medical men of the city.

CHAPTER TWENTY-FOUR

Willie's Plans Bear Fruit

When his studies were finished, Willie returned to assist his father, for he had no desire to settle in a great city and become a fashionable doctor, getting large fees and growing rich. He regarded the purpose of his life as being, in a large measure, just to take his share in the general business.

By this time the reputation of the Prior's Well had spread on all sides, and the country people had begun to visit the Leas, and stay for a week or ten days to drink the water. Indeed, so many kept coming and going through the garden that the MacMichaels finally found it troublesome, and had a small pipe laid to a little stone trough built into the garden wall on the outside, so that whoever would, might come and drink with less trouble to all concerned.

But Willie had come home with a new idea in his head.

An old valetudinarian* in the city, who knew every spa in Europe, wanted to try that of Priory Leas, and had consulted him about it. Finding that there was no such accommodation to be had as he judged suitable, he seriously advised Willie and his father to build a house fit for persons of position (as he called them), assuring him that they would soon make their fortunes if they did. Now although this was not the ambition of either father or son, for a fortune had never seemed to either worth taking trouble about, yet it suggested something that was better.

"Why," said Willie to his father, "shouldn't we restore a bit of the Priory in such a way that a man like Mr. Yellowley could endure it for a little while? He would pay us well, and then we should be able to do more for those who can't pay us."

"We couldn't cook for a man like that," said his mother.

"He wouldn't want that," said his father. "He would be sure to bring his own servants."

Dr. MacMichael thought the thing worth trying, and resolved to lay out all his little savings, as well as what Willie could add, on getting a kitchen and a few convenient rooms constructed in the ruins, keeping as much as possible to their original plan and architectural character. He found, however, that it would take a thousand pounds—a good deal more than they could scrape together between them. He was on the point of giving up the scheme, or at least altering it for one that would have been much longer in making them any return, when Mr. Shepherd, who had become acquainted with their plans, and consequently with their difficulties, offered to join them with the little he had laid aside for a rainy day—which proved just sufficient to complete the sum necessary. Between the three the thing was effected, and Mr. Yellowley was their first visitor.

He grumbled a good deal at first at the proximity of the cobbler, and at having to meet him in his walks about the garden—but this was a point on which Dr. MacMichael, who of course took the old man's complaints good-humoredly, would not budge, and he had to reconcile himself to it as he best might. Before long they became excellent friends, for if you will only give time and opportunity to an ordinarily good man, his nature will overcome in the end. Mr. Yellowley was at heart good-natured, and the cobbler was well worth knowing. Before the former left, the two were often to be seen pacing the garden together and talking happily.

Mr. Yellowley was wonderfully restored by the air and the water and the medical care of Dr. MacMichael, and when he went away after nearly six months, he paid a hundred and fifty pounds—a good return in six months for the outlay of a thousand pounds. This they saved to accumulate for the next addition, and by various gradations of growth, room after room arose from the ruins of the Priory. And the Priory, having once taken to growing, went on with it. They cleared away mound after mound from the garden, turning them once more into solid walls, for they were formed mainly of excellent stones, which had just been waiting to be put up again. The garden became a little less picturesque by their removal, although, on the other hand, a good deal more productive.

And the Priory spread as well as grew, until it encroached upon the garden. But for this a remedy soon appeared.

The next house and garden, although called the Manse, were Mr. Shepherd's own property. The ruins formed a great part of the boundary between the two, and it was plain to see that the Priory had once extended a good way into what was now the other garden. Indeed Mr. Shepherd's house, as well as Dr. MacMichael's, had been built out of the ruins. Mr. Shepherd offered to have the wall torn down and the building extended on his side of the wall as well, so that it should stand in the middle of one large garden.

The question as to what would have become of it if the two proprietors had quarreled was unnecessary, for it had become less likely than ever that such a thing should happen in the future. Willie had told Mona that he loved her more than he could tell, and wanted to ask her a question, only he didn't know how. And Mona had told Willie that she would suppose his question if he would suppose her answer, and Willie had said, "May I suppose it to be the very answer I should like?" and Mona had answered "Yes!" quite decidedly, and Willie had given her a kiss, and Mona had taken the kiss and given him another for it. And so it was all understood, and there was no fear of the wall having to be built up again between the gardens.

So the Priory grew and flourished and gained great reputation, and the fame of the two doctors, father and son,
spread far and wide for the cures they wrought. And many
people came and paid them large sums—but the more rich
people that came, the more poor people the MacMichaels
invited. For they never would allow the making of money to
intrude upon the dignity of their high calling. How should
avarice and cure go together? *A greedy healer of men!* What
a marriage of words!

The Priory became quite a grand building. The chapel
grew up again, and had windows of stained glass that shone
like jewels. Mr. Shepherd preached in the parish church in
the morning, and preached in the Priory chapel on the
Sunday evening—and all the patients, and anyone besides
that pleased, went there to hear him.

They built great baths, hot and cold, and of all kinds—
from baths where people could swim, to baths where they
were only showered on by a very sharp rain. It was a great
and admirable place, well suited to be the full fruit of
Willie's dream.

In later years, after Dr. MacMichael and Mr. Shepherd had
died, Mona had a picture of Willie's dream painted, with
portraits of the two men as the two angels.

GLOSSARY

adze: A woodworker's tool used to shape the surface of wood; its blade is curved, and set at right angles to the handle.

aurora borealis: A shimmering curtain of colored lights which can sometimes be seen in the northern sky. (Also called Northern Lights.)

baize: A coarse woolen fabric generally used for curtains and coverings.

bodkin: A small pointed tool used for making holes in cloth or leather.

bradawl: An awl used to make holes to hold brads.

bugbear: An imaginary, threatening, bear-shaped hobgoblin; any source of unnecessary fear.

chintz: Cotton cloth, often printed with flowered designs

damask: Rich silk or linen fabric with elaborate and colorful designs.

dock-stalk: The stalk of the common dock weed, frequently plucked and applied to soothe the pain of nettle-stings.

earnest: Money paid to guarantee a contract or bargain.

gobble-stitch: Careless or sloppy stitch-work.

gudgeon blocks: Blocks used to hold the gudgeons, or pivots, applied to the ends of the waterwheel axles.

joists: Large, sturdy beams used to support the floors of houses.

lathe: A machine used for shaping wood and metal; the

material is made to rotate against a fixed cutting or shaping tool.

lichens: Small gray, green, or yellow plants found on rocks or trees.

muffettees: A woolen cuff intended to be worn around the wrist.

peat: A thick mossy layer of decayed plants which forms peat bogs. In Scotland, peat was often cut into small pieces, dried, and burned as fuel.

priory: A monastery governed by a prior.

punch: A hardened tool used to make holes in metal or wood or leather or masonry; a hammer is generally used to force the punch through the material.

quick-lime: A preparation of lime which can be used to make mortar.

refectory: The dining hall or room in a religious institution.

ricks: A stack of hay or corn.

rove: To weave or rig a rope through a set or system of pulleys.

shakedown: A makeshift bed made from loose straw mounded on the floor.

shilling: A silver coin worth twelve pennies (or two sixpence).

sixpence: A silver coin worth six pennies (or half a shilling).

slate: A thin, flat piece of gray stone (resembling a small blackboard) carried by schoolchildren and used as an erasable writing tablet.

sluice: An adjustable gate used to control the flow of water in a channel.

sovereign: A gold coin worth twenty shillings.

spirit-level: A tool used to level a piece of material during construction. The level itself has a clear sealed cylinder mostly filled with liquid; the bubble of air left in the cylinder is used to determine if the tool is being held level.

turner: A craftsman who operates a lathe (or potter's wheel).

valetudinarian: An invalid (or person in poor health) who is obsessed with his or her own ailments.

Winner Books are produced by Victor Books and are designed to entertain and instruct young readers in Christian principles.

Other Winner Books you will enjoy:
The Mystery Man of Horseshoe Bend
  by Linda Boorman
The Drugstore Bandit of Horseshoe Bend
  by Linda Boorman
The Hairy Brown Angel and Other Animal Tails
  edited by Grace Fox Anderson
The Peanut Butter Hamster and Other Animal Tails
  edited by Grace Fox Anderson
Skunk for Rent and Other Animal Tails
  edited by Grace Fox Anderson
The Incompetent Cat and Other Animal Tails
  edited by Grace Fox Anderson
The Duck Who Had Goosebumps and Other Animal Tails
  edited by Grace Fox Anderson
The Mysterious Prowler by Frances Carfi Matranga
The Forgotten Treasure by Frances Carfi Matranga
The Mystery of the Missing Will by Frances Carfi Matranga
The Hair-Pulling Bear Dog by Lee Roddy
The City Bear's Adventures by Lee Roddy
Dooger, the Grasshopper Hound by Lee Roddy
The Ghost Dog of Stoney Ridge by Lee Roddy
Mad Dog of Lobo Mountain by Lee Roddy
The Legend of the White Raccoon by Lee Roddy
The Boyhood of Ranald Bannerman by George MacDonald
The Genius of Willie MacMichael by George MacDonald
The Wanderings of Clare Skymer by George MacDonald

Dear Reader:

We would like to know your thoughts about the book you've just read. Your ideas will help us as we seek to publish books that will interest you.

Send your responses to: **WINNER BOOKS**
1825 College Avenue
Wheaton, IL 60187

What made you decide to read The Genius of Willie MacMichael?

☐ I bought it for myself

☐ My parents bought it for me.

☐ It was a gift.

☐ It was part of a school assignment.

☐ It was loaned to me by a friend.

What did you like most about this book? (You can check more than one answer.)

☐ Characters
☐ Story
☐ Mystery
☐ Animals
☐ Romance

☐ Adventure
☐ Humor
☐ Inside art sketches
☐ Glossary
☐ Other: _____

From the following list, please check the subjects you would like to read about in the future. (You can check more than one answer.)

☐ Sports
☐ Make-believe
☐ Science fiction
☐ Animals
☐ Real people
☐ History

☐ Scary stories
☐ Mysteries
☐ Comics
☐ Devotional books
☐ Other: _____

Would you be interested in reading other Winner books?
(Check only one answer.)

☐ Very interested   ☐ Not at all interested
☐ A little bit interested

Would you pass along this book to a friend?

☐ YES   ☐ NO

How old are you?

☐ Under 8   ☐ 11
☐ 8   ☐ 12
☐ 9   ☐ Over 12
☐ 10

Would you be interested in a Winner book club? If so, please fill in your name and address below:

NAME: _____

ADDRESS: _____

_____

WINNER BOOKS BY GEORGE MACDONALD

The Boyhood of Ranald Bannerman

This is the story of George MacDonald's Scottish childhood, thinly disguised as fiction. Ranald Bannerman chronicles his childhood from his very first memories through to the point where he "becomes a man" by confronting death. Edited for today's young readers by Dan Hamilton (6-2748).

The Genius of Willie MacMichael

Willie MacMichael is a mechanical genius who masters every trade and skill he sets his hand to. Through his talents, Willie creatively learns to serve other people. Edited for today's young readers by Dan Hamilton (6-2750).

The Wanderings of Clare Skymer

A devastating earthquake leaves young Clare Skymer homeless and starts him on his wanderings. He endures hunger and hard times—and his adventures lead him to bulls and bears, pachyderms and pumas, bakers and blacksmiths, ladies and lions, and tramps and thieves. Edited for today's young readers (6-2757).

THE EXITORN ADVENTURES

Visit the make-believe kingdom of Exitorn where you'll meet 12-year-old Brill and his daredevil friend, Segra. Their fast-paced fantasy stories will keep you turning the pages to see what will happen next.

Brill and the Dragators

Brill longs for his humble home when he is brought to the palace as a companion to the crown prince. The emperor and his son live only for pleasure and Brill remembers how different they are from his grandfather who lives for God. Will Brill and Segra be able to help the former king escape from prison? (6-1344)

Segra and Stargull

Segra and Brill journey through Exitorn, across stormy seas, and into a neighboring country seeking Segra's parents. Their adventures call for courage and faith as time and again Segra risks her life and Brill's to help someone in need (6-1345).

Segra in Diamond Castle

Segra is kidnapped and held prisoner by Umber in Diamond Castle. When her escape attempts fail, she comes up with a plan to outsmart Umber and end his war with Exitorn (6-1449).

Brill and the Zinders

Brill and Segra travel to Magra to locate the Zinders. Only the tiny Zinders can brew the special medicine needed to cure the plague that's spreading through Exitorn. But Prince Jaspin of Magra is also searching for the tiny dwarfs. Can Brill and Segra find the Zinders and protect them from the sneaky prince? (6-1450)